Collegiate Expectations

Teaching the Millennial Generation

Written by

Chrystal Denmark Porter, Ph.D., Ed.S.

College Strategies Books
Longview, Texas

Published in 2007 by

College Strategies Books
513 Honeysuckle Lane, Longview, TX 75605
World Wide Web: www.CollegeStrategiesOnline.com
E-mail: Chrystal@TheCollegePro.com

Collegiate expectations: teaching the millennial generation / Chrystal Denmark Porter—1st ed.

Includes bibliographical references and index.

ISBN 978-0-6151-5050-5

1. College students—United States. 2. Millennial generation—United States. 3. College teaching
Prevention. I. Porter, Chrystal Denmark, 1975-

First edition, 2007

ISBN 978-0-6151-5050-5: paperback

Printed in the United States of America.

Acknowledgments

I am grateful to all my friends, family, colleagues, and students who helped me gain the confidence, knowledge, and perseverance to make this book a reality, including:

The Lord God Almighty, who blesses me, keeps me curious, and keeps me safe. Thank you for helping me learn the lessons I need to learn, and helping me find the path I need to take.

My beautiful daughter Maya, my inspiration. I will always be your example.

James and Barbara Denmark, you have and continue to prove to be the best parents anyone could ask for. Thank you for everything that you have done for me through the years. You have allowed me the opportunity to love life and learning. Thank you for being so supportive and understanding in all my ventures.

Christopher Denmark, thank you for being the best big brother anyone could ask for. You have always believed in me and my potential and I thank you of reminding me of it. You and I were put here to do important work, and both of us are well on the way of achieving that goal.

Brian Porter, my best friend and husband. Thank you so much for believing in me through the years. I have walked down several paths, and yet you stood beside me even when you did not have to. You are my heart, and with you I can accomplish almost everything.

Deserea Russell, thank you for such a wonderful friendship. You have helped me learn so much about myself, and how to figure out the ups-and-downs of this thing we call life. I wish you equal success in all your endeavors.

This book is dedicated to all my ancestors. I would not be who I am without their successes and struggles.

Preface

The theoretical research about the millennial generation, specifically millennial generation college students, is growing in popularity (Howe and Strauss, 2000; Howe and Strauss, 2003; Oblinger, 2003; Pascarella and Terenzini, 1998). Although millennial age students have been enrolling in colleges for the past few years, there remains limited research about how educational institutions and individual instructors can reasonably meet the needs of their students while appropriately resisting trends or practices that may compromise the quality of instruction to which their students are entitled.

College instructors, in particular, face unique challenges in the contemporary college environment. Using traditional methods to design a course and deliver course content through a traditional lecture format may not in many cases be the best method instructors should use if they are truly interested in the students learning process (Oblinger, 2003). As student bodies continue to diversify and student expectations about college continue to evolve and expand, it might be advantageous for college instructors to examine the complexities of the students they are teaching.

First, understanding how students view their general positions or roles within higher education can help reveal what students believe their goals are in attending college. For example, students may have the expectation that education owes them in some manner for participating in the higher learning process. According to Sacks (1996),

> For consumers who buy an education, the notion of success is increasingly treated as a quasi-negotiable exchange; you pay your money and get what you pay for, regardless of what you put into the deal. Indeed, some consumers of education seem to invest no more

personal responsibility in the transaction than a
McDonald's customer buying a Quarter Pounder with
cheese. (p. 156)

Second, this study allows for exploration in understanding the
topic of entitlement. Sacks (1996) reported that students may be more
adept to believe that they are entitled to certain experiences while
attending their postsecondary institution. The sense of entitlement
may be viewed as an extension of the perceptions that students view
themselves as consumers. As more colleges and universities
implement business-like strategies to attract students to their
institutions, students are becoming more keenly aware of their return-
on-investment (Levine & Cureton, 1998; Spiegler, 1998).

Third, more information can be obtained in relation to the role
entertainment plays in education today. In a survey of his college
students, Sacks (1996) asked his students to identify what personal
characteristics they valued in a college teacher. Among the top three
choices identified by the students were that the instructor be
entertaining, friendly and warm, and challenging. Many college
students today have grown up watching television and ultimately
place a higher value on being entertained (Sacks, 1996).

Sacks (1996) suggested that educators reassess their
commitment to education and the emerging standards for enlivening
course curricula. He wrote:

In what appears to be an increasingly common
sentiment within higher education, the author of one
educational journal article concluded: 'If effective
teachers are entertaining teachers, and today's media-
saturated students expect to be entertained and cannot
tolerate boredom, then it is time to underscore the need
for entertainment in the classroom.' (p. 147)

The term *edutainment* has been coined to describe
phenomenon of combining traditional education with
entertaining activities. There is a growing group of instructors
who purposefully intend to provide entertaining activities as a
means to relay information to their students. Contemporary

trends in higher education may also support edutainment, not for its value in educating college students, however it can be used as a means for the institution to better market themselves and attract prospective students.

The modern system of higher education is marketed with many new features and ideas. The salient features of education in the new age are: an open and flexible system, direct and easy access to every learner, a broad based and futuristic visionary stream of learning, edutainment and infotainment and student-centered learning, that is more emphasis on insight and knowledge than mere information collection, new knowledge with a personal touch and need and utility-oriented learning (Popli, 2005, p. 18).

It is to be assumed that if students were adequately motivated in their classes, the result would be twofold. First, students would have enhanced collegiate academic experiences that encourages one to learn more. Second, certain instructional problems that exist between instructors and students might be resolved.

Contents

Chapter 1

Introduction

Background of the Study

Traditionally, the term *generation* is used to define groups of individuals born within a 20-year duration (Beller, Weiss, & Patler, 2005). Researchers Levine and Cureton (1998) further indicate that a generation can result from a group incurring common momentous experiences. However, there has not been a generation as populous as the "Millennial Generation," those born after 1982, since the historical population boom that took place in the 1950s and 1960s with the "Baby Boomer Generation." Between 1982 and 2002, there were over 81.5 million births (Hobbs & Nicole, 2002). The boomers' overwhelming size and relevant moment in history placed them in position to modify the status quo common within the American society.

"'Baby Boomers' grew up with the space race, the civil rights movement, Vietnam, and Watergate. Generation X saw the fall of the Berlin Wall and the emergence of AIDS and the Web" (Oblinger, 2003, p. 38). The millennials are coming of age in a post-9/11, post-Columbine, instant messaging, Web-surfing, and blog writing society. Noted millennial generation researchers Howe and Strauss (2000, 2003) report on how the significant changes that occur in the larger society continue to influence the life experience of the millennial generation, and they also define how the generation's culture will function quite differently from previous generations. "…Millennials are growing up to embody a *sharp break* from Gen-X youth trends and a *direct reversal* of Boomer youth trends" (Howe & Strauss, 2000, p. 28).

As the group matures and their culture develops, trend watchers are interested in characterizing the facets that are unique to this generation. According to Howe and Strauss (2000):

> As a group, Millennials are unlike any other youth generation in living memory. They are more numerous, more affluent, better educated, and more ethnically diverse. More important they are beginning to manifest a wide array of positive social habits that older Americans no longer associate with youth, including a new focus on teamwork, achievement, modesty, and good conduct. Only a few years from now, this can-do youth revolution will overwhelm the cynics and pessimists. Over the next decade, the Millennial Generation will entirely recast the image of youth from downbeat and alienated to upbeat and engaged—with potentially seismic consequences for America. (p. 4)

Although college campuses have catered to students who are classified as millennial-age students for the past few years, institutions of higher education are entering an era where they cannot ignore experiencing these students' unique qualities, idiosyncrasies, and influences. "The largest part of the millennial generation bubble has already begun to hit colleges and will reach its peak between 2005 and 2011" (Knight, 2003).

Millennial generation college students are well versed in the advantages that a college education can provide. More than any other generation, the millennials are entering academic institutions far more sophisticated, demanding and technologically skilled. These students are entering college with high expectations and well formed, preconceived ideas about the experiences they should have while in college, including the experiences they should have within their academic courses. "Millennials expect to be able to choose what kind of education they buy, and what, where, and how they learn" (Carlson, 2005, A34).

Some colleges and some instructors, who have acknowledged the shift in the culture, report that they are making adjustments to enhance the learning experiences of their millennial population students. Carlson (2005) suggested that contemporary college students approach learning very differently than their predecessors. Specifically, the millennials have incorporated into their learning collaborative groups, laptops, e-mail, Instant Message, and subject specific computer software.

However, within the academy, there are many educators who relentlessly continue on as they always have, oblivious or unconcerned of the transforming expectations of their students (Carlson, 2005). Some faculty and administrators are unconvinced that the millennials ability to learn is different from other groups. There is the assertion that students desire only to employ enhanced learning technologies and instruction methods after they have been revealed to them by their instructors, rather than because of an initial desire for them. According to Carlson (2005),

> Administrators push professors to use technology in the classroom because they believe that is what today's students want...And faculty members feel pressured to shorten lectures, increase group-discussion time, and ignore the 'multitasking' student who is emailing his friends in the back of the room— all to attract and satisfy a generation that doesn't have the discipline of its predecessors. (p. A35)

Institutions that miss out on the trends that are developing among their traditional aged students may severely impact the status and stature of an institution in the long-term. Researchers Howe and Strauss (2003) believed that ignoring the demands and desires of the millennial generation could be a huge mistake. "Colleges and universities that figure out the new trends, make wise tuition and budget choices, and market intelligently to today's youth, will be able to 're-brand' their own reputations, leapfrog rivals—and, perhaps, join the top echelons of academe". (Howe & Strauss, 2003, p. 5)

Although experts continue to report on the demands the millennial generation has after they are in college (Carlson, 2005; Howe & Strauss, 2003; Howe & Strauss, 2000; Knight, 2003; Oblinger, 2003), limited resources are available to clarify what students truly expect from faculty, and more specifically, their learning experiences. There is growing support for institutions and instructors to use developing technologies, such as online course-management systems, or courses that are modified to integrate audio, video, or interactive components, and collaborative learning activities to enhance student learning (Baiocco & Bilken, 1998, Dortch, 1997, Fink, 2003, Sacks, 1996). Yet to what degree should college students play in dictating how they should learn and how far their institutions and instructors should go to meet their needs? This question will be difficult to answer if there is little information about whether the students or the institutions are the truly the more influential group.

Purpose of the Study

The purpose of this study was to describe the expectations that millennial generation students have regarding their collegiate experiences, focusing on student responses about student-faculty interaction and course learning. The study identified similar responses and common experiences described by the students interviewed, and highlighted statements that captured and summarized major themes.

Research Question

Consistent with qualitative study research design, the leading research question was broad in nature to allow the methodology to emerge and evolve (Bogdan & Biklen, 1998). The primary research question under the phenomenological format was "stated broadly without specific reference to the existing literature or a typology of questions…" (Creswell, 1994, pp. 70-71).

The study attempted to address the following research question: What does it mean to millennial generation college students when they compare their actual collegiate learning experiences with what they anticipated? College students between the ages of 18 and 22 will be asked a series of unscripted questions so they can describe their collegiate academic experiences. The researcher examined the responses provided by the students from in-depth interviews.

4

Researcher Assumptions and Limitations

There were three underlying assumptions. First, it was assumed that the participants would provide honest responses duration of the study. Second, the researcher assumed the researcher would ask probing questions that would generate valuable information from the respondents. The final assumption was that the researcher would identify for the reader any personal biases that could affect her interpretation of the participant's responses.

There were two limitations with this study. First, the input provided by the participants of this study were their individual, personal opinions and impression. The participant's responses in the study were not generalizable and may not have reflected the points of views of other individuals or the entire generation. Second, the conclusions of the study could be subject to other interpretations. The author's intent was to present a fair and accurate description of the information shared by the participants.

Nature of the Study

This was a qualitative research study. A qualitative research format was selected by the researcher as a means to allow the study's participants the opportunity to describe, in their own words, what they anticipated college academic would entail, and express what they had experienced. A qualitative study typically involves a research process that will generate understanding to a question based on "building a complex, holistic picture, formed with words, reporting detailed views of informants, and conducted in a natural setting" (Creswell, 1994, p.2). The phenomenological qualitative format was chosen because this method systematically examines a small number of individuals so the researcher can successfully to develop understanding about the tangible or evident experiences of the participants.

Chapter 2

College Student Demographics

The term *"college student"* has never before been used to characterize such a diverse group of individuals than it does today. The description—heterosexual, white, male, ages 18 to 22, who attends a four-year institution for four years while maintaining a full course load and living in a campus dormitory—no longer distinguishes the vast majority of individuals enrolled in institutions of higher education in the United States (Levine & Cureton, 1998; Pascarella & Terenzini, 1998; Speer, 1996). Instead today's college student bodies are comprised of a wide range of persons who come from different backgrounds and experiences and share little in common with one another other than that they are all interested in pursuing post-secondary educational opportunities.

Legal mandates have historically been the primary influencing factors that motivated post-secondary institutions ultimately to establish new policies and practices resulting in a more diverse student body. In the last century, a number of significant laws, statutes, and executive orders were instrumental in expanding opportunities to diverse groups of individuals in the realm of higher education. Significant mandates included the following:

1. Executive Order 11246 (as amended by Executive Order 11375) mandates the utility of affirmative action;

2. Title VII of the Civil Rights Act of 1964, as amended, prohibit discrimination in employment on the basis of race, color, religion, sex or national origin;

3. Title IX of the Elementary, Secondary Act of 1972, the first legislation precluding discrimination against

students on the basis of sex and also include some aspects of employment;

4. Title VI of the Civil Rights Act of 1964, prohibits discrimination on the basis of race, color, or national origin;

5. Section 503 of the Rehabilitation Act of 1973, prohibits discrimination on the basis of handicaps;

6. Age Discrimination in the Employment Act of 1967, as amended prohibit discrimination of the basis of age;

7. Equal Pay Act of 1963, as amended, prohibit differential pay rates for women and men doing the same work; and

8. Pregnancy Discrimination Act of 1978, amending Title VII, declares that pregnant women shall be regarded one and the same for all employment related purposes as other persons not affected by similar ability or inability (Pearson, Shavlik, & Touchton, 1989, p. 4).

The repercussions that the aforementioned mandates have had on college campuses continue to influence the patterns and trends that occur within contemporary student bodies. Significant changes are related to student ethnic, gender and enrollment status make-up. For a large proportion of college instructors, considering their student demographics when developing course curriculums, learning activities, and teaching strategies may prove to be especially advantageous in addressing challenges they may encounter with students.

Ethnicity

White students traditionally have dominated the largest ethnic group attending college in the United States, embodying 80.5 % of the present day student population (The Chronicle of Higher Education, 2005). American academic culture initially evolved from a conceptual model that extensively catered and made accommodations for members of the dominate culture. Values and ideals of the dominate culture often are reflected in institutional policies and class procedures. Some instructors may be unaware that they are perpetuating a method that could be favorable to one group over another because college policies and teaching are often perpetuated out of long- standing tradition and comfort.

Historically, African-Americans have been the largest minority group that had to learn to maneuver in an established academic system (Taylor, 1997). In 1865, the Freedman's Bureau was established by an act of Congress to aid the newly emancipated slaves in the South. From 1865 to 1872, the governmental agency was responsible for assisting with the development of a school system for African-Americans. By the conclusion of its operation, the Bureau, in conjunction with church related missionary societies and other private non-secular northern groups, successfully helped to establish 4,300 schools at the primary, secondary, and post-secondary levels, including more than 200 historically Black colleges and universities (Brown II, 2001).

For most African-Americans before the Civil Rights Movement and the mandatory elimination of segregation in higher education, historically Black colleges and universities (HBCUs) provided the only opportunity for many individuals fortunate enough to pursue a college education (Taylor, 1997). Currently many African-American collegians continue to pursue their post-secondary degree work at HBCUs; however, the vast majority of the near 2,000,000 African-Americans attending college are attending institutions where the student bodies have been and continue to be predominantly white (Brown, 2001; The Chronicle of Higher Education, 2005).

There has also been a steady increase in the number of Asian, Hispanic, and American Indian collegians. These groups represent 6%, 10%, and 1% of college students respectively (The Chronicle of Higher Education, 2005). In addition, there are approximately 590,900 international students coming from such countries as China, Japan, the Republic of Korea, India, Taiwan, Canada, Thailand, Indonesia, Malaysia, and Mexico, totaling around four percent of the United States college student population.

The importance of recognizing and addressing the relevance of diverse classrooms remains a meaningful topic in conversations related to higher education. Brown (2004) writes:

> Over the past several decades, issues of diversity have moved from their peripheral positions to become central concerns of institutions of higher education. Fostering this transition has been a range of policy decisions and program implementations specifically aimed at (a) increasing the number of persons that represent diverse populations, and (b) improving the climate that would sustain the population. (p. 21)

Gender composition

As early as the colonial era of American history, possibilities for women to pursue educational opportunities freely were limited. Originally, institutions of higher education in the United States were established as seminaries that were initially utilized by young, white men from privileged families who could afford to send their sons to college. It was widely argued and accepted during this time that any formal education for women was not only unsuitable, but might even be damaging (McClelland, 1992; Miller-Bernal, 2000).

It would not be until the mid- to late nineteenth century that more opportunities become available for women in higher education (McClelland, 1992; Pearson et al, 1989). During this time, several women's colleges were established and designed to accommodate the needs and interests of their female student bodies. Similar to their male counterparts, women's colleges provided advantages to women pursing professional careers; however, the majority of women who attended the schools were from privileged, upper-class backgrounds (McClelland, 1992; Miller-Bernal, 2000).

Where women were accepted into coeducational institutions of higher education prior to the 1970s, many encountered quandaries of being regarded differently than the male students, and many were victims of what may best be characterized as discriminatory practices (McClelland, 1992). In the late 1960s and early 1970s, issues related to sex discrimination in education gained momentum with bills and proposals being made by members of Congress to outlaw such

10

activity. Title IX of the Education Amendments of 1972 was passed into law as a means to prohibit sex discrimination in any educational institutions or agency receiving federal funding.

> There is a sense in which Title IX, at the time of its adoption…simply captured what was an independence social norm of considerable force. Women were participating in higher education…in increasing numbers and were properly claiming a right to equal opportunity. (Weistart, 1996, p. 29)

Since Title IX and other Civil Rights mandates have been introduced into legislation, more females are successfully completing secondary, post-secondary, graduate, and professional degrees at an all-time record number (The Chronicle of Higher Education, 2005). Prior to the legislation of the 1960s and the 1970s, the number of women attending college fluctuated. In 1900, approximately 85,000 women enrolled in some type of post-secondary institution, representing 36.8 percent of all college students (McClelland, 1992). By the 1920s, women comprised approximately 47% of the college student population, and this was the first time in American history when the number of women attending post-secondary institutions was relatively comparable to their male counterparts (McClelland, 1992). However, the number of women attending college over the duration of and after World War II greatly decreased. Not until after the Civil Rights and Women's Movements were introduced did the number of women attending college in the United States make steady gains and once again equal to or exceeded the number of men registered in college.

As of the fall 2002 academic school year with 9,409,600 people enrolled, women embodied approximately 57% of the student population (The Chronicle of Higher Education, 2005). Often described as the "new majority" in the educational spectrum, the women who attend post-secondary institutions are quite diverse in terms of their ages, social classes, race, ethnicity, and religious affiliations (Pearson et al., 1997; Speer, 1996).

Enrollment Status

As more demands, both personal and scholastic, are being placed on college students, more students are opting to decrease the amount of commitment they are making to attend college. In 1996, virtually half of college students, over 6.6 million, were attending college on a part-time basis, up from 3 million who were enrolled as part-time students in 1970 (Leveine & Cureton, 1998; Pascarella & Terenzini, 1998).

According to Dortch (1997), there is a direct correlation between part-time college enrollment increasing and periods of high unemployment. However, even in a moderately stable economy, more students are deciding not to matriculate through post-secondary degree programs using the previous standards that assume the student should attend every term with full course loads. Instead more students are merging their educational pursuits into their personal and employment plans (Levine & Cureton, 1998; Speer, 1996).

Student employment is another well-documented change with the overall student population. A substantial number of students regularly attend classes while also being employed. "In 1993, 46 percent of all full-time college students ages 18 to 24 were employed, and more than half of those worked at least 20 hours per week" (Pascarella & Terenzini, 1998 p. 157). In 1998 an estimated 54 percent of all students in college were employed (Levine & Cureton, 1998).

Until the latter half of the twentieth century, most individuals who attended post-secondary institutions were primarily able to do so through the financial support provided by their families. Accordingly, a number of the men and women enrolled in colleges and universities were from fairly wealthy lineages (McClelland, 1992; Miller-Bernal, 2000). It was not until after World War II and the introduction of the GI Bill, which provided financial aid to United States servicemen for college tuition and living expenses, that more economically diverse groups were able to afford a post-secondary education (Cohen & Brawer, 1996). Over time governmental grants and loans continued to provide financial assistance to students and their families who may not otherwise have been able to afford fees associated with attending post-secondary institutions.

Among the financial aid alternatives provided by several colleges and universities for students included the Federal Work-Study Financial Aid Program. The program was designed specifically to have students work while attending classes. Although limitations are specified about the total number of hours a week that students can work at their jobs and about the number of hours a student may enroll for each semester of course work, work-study has become a viable means for many students requiring financial assistance to earn additional monies for personal and educational purposes. The Chronicle of Higher Education (2005) reported that approximately 892,000 college students actively participated as a work-study student.

There is also a steady trend of non-traditional adult students returning to post-secondary institutions in significant numbers. Many of these students are attending classes while maintaining some type of employment. For some adult students, taking post-secondary coursework is not only a means to receive a degree, but also attending college classes may be necessary for the individuals to be able to keep a job and/or remain current in the information related to their position or industry (Speer, 1998).

Chapter 3

College Student Attitudes

The influence that the changing society has had on the college student population has been the theme of various research studies (Bennet-Johnson, 1997; Di, 1996; Hashway, 1996; Levine & Cureton, 1998; Spigler, 1998; Tang & Zuo, 1997). Results from different studies revealed that contemporary college students are, in fact, greatly affected by the culture economically, politically, socially, and psychologically (Levine & Cureton, 1998). There are distinct factors with which today's college students must deal that could interfere with their ability academically to achieve (Di, 1996).

Stressed

Today's college students are distressed and suspicious about their economic prospects after they graduate and depart college (Levine & Cureton, 1998). Students are concerned about being able to find employment after college that will provide them with enough security to function properly and independently of their parents or government related support. Although students openly acknowledge that in order to achieve a successful career they may be required to work numerous hours in their positions out of college they indicated that they would like to spend less of their time in college studying and doing homework (Spiegler, 1998).

Students are also expressing concerns related to their personal safety. "The rapes, theft, assault, vandalism, and murder crimes of the nation, are beginning to spill over into the college and university campus" (Bennett-Johnson, 1997). More students, specifically women, are greatly concerned about the likelihood of being the victim of an offence not only while maneuvering through society but also while on a college campus (Bennett-Johnson, 1997; Levine & Cureton, 1998).

Disappointed

College students are aware of a large proportion of the matters that plague not only the American society but also the world community (e.g. poverty, racism, crime, pollution, global conflict). Many do not harbor the opinion that these issues will be suitably resolved in their lifetimes or through political agendas or governmental agencies. College students tend to have a somewhat pessimistic attitude about what or who will have the capability to bring change or solution successfully to many of the major issues affecting the society at large (Levine & Cureton, 1998).

However, college students, in general, do accept that they can help bring about change to their immediate situations and that they have social and civic responsibility. Research indicates that students are involved in activities that could positively impact their communities and neighborhoods. Approximately two-thirds of undergraduate students participate or have participated in voluntary activities and two-thirds are registered to vote (Hashway, 1996; Levine & Cureton, 1998).

Unstructured Activities

One-third of college students indicated that they have no time for an active social life or time or interest to participate voluntarily in organized activities (Levine & Cureton, 1998). There is evidence that fewer students are involved in organizations registered with their institution, including Greek-life organizations. "More people are doing things individually and in separate groups than campus wide" (Student Affairs Survey, 1997, as cited in Levine & Cureton, 1998, p. 102).

Many students reported that they, in general, are fatigued. Research (Levine & Cureton, 1998) looking at how students prioritize their time indicated how students divide their time could impact the quality of their higher educational experience. Many of today's college students revealed they consider "sleeping" as a form of recreation (Levine & Cureton, 1998). One research study (Spiegler,

1997) indicated although students spend approximately 17.4 hours and 14.8 hours a week in class and studying, respectively, the students ranked sleeping as the number one activity in which they are engaged, spending approximately 44 hours doing just that (Soper, Kelly, & Von Bergen, 1997).

Students also reported that they are more inclined to have fun in the club-and-bar scene (Levine & Cureton, 1998). Consequently, more students are engaging in drinking and drug related activities, although at varied degrees of usage.

Worried About Academics

Most students do enthusiastically credit that they are working hard when characterizing their personal commitment to their academics. One report states:

> Only 7 percent of undergraduates say they don't care what grades they receive. Although they express a good deal of ambivalence about how accurately grades reflect their achievements (saying it is possible to get good grades without understanding the material)…Undergraduates told us they wanted to get high grades and felt great pressure to get them. (Levine & Cureton, 1998, p. 124)

Coincidentally, academic dishonesty continues to be a serious problem plaguing many American campuses. Students of all ethnicities, ages, and socio-economic classes are reporting that they have engaged in some classification of cheating while attending college. Studies implied that approximately 39 percent of college students have engaged in some form of cheating (Tang & Zuo, 1997).

It should also be noted that more students are beginning to regard higher educational institutions with consumer mentalities. As more colleges and universities successfully implement business-like strategies to attract students to their institutions, students are expecting schools to live up to their promises and guarantee a return-on-investment (Levine & Cureton, 1998; Spiegler, 1998).

17

College students are also becoming more disengaged with college. Speigler (1998) reported that an exploratory survey of the freshmen class of 2001 revealed that approximately 36% of the students had been "bored" while attending classes, approximately 35% missed class as a result of oversleeping, and only 34% mentioned that they studied more than six hours per week.

Special

Another area the millennials differ than their generational predecessors involves their perception that others should recognize and acknowledge their unique attributes, skills, situation, and differences. In addition, others should be compassionate to their unique and special qualities and allow them the opportunity to experience all things they believe they are entitled, even if no other individual has or will receive the same treatment or opportunity.

The idea that most millennials perceive themselves as special has often been the result of over-reaching parents who regularly communicate through their actions and words what their child should be entitled. The term *helicopter parents* has been used to describe millennial parents. Helicopter parents are "always hovering— ultraprotctive, unwilling to let go, enlisting 'the team' (physician, lawyer, psychiatrist, professional counselors) to assert a variety of special needs and interests" (Howe & Strauss, 2003, p. 11).

Some college campuses have responded to this trend in their promotional materials and services. Many colleges attempt to highlight for prospective students and their parents how their institution can address what makes them special, ranging from academic giftedness to learning disabilities, all the while allowing the student an opportunity to be a unique member of the campus community.

> …[S]pecialness implies that every student be congratulated frequently for his or her progress through the curriculum. This requires programs to be carefully and regularly monitored, problems dealt with promptly or even preemptively, and no student allowed to fall by the wayside. The 'no child left behind' approach that Millennials have experienced in grades

K through 12 makes them expect that the difficulty of the subject matter will always be properly geared to each student's ability. (Howe & Strauss, 2003, p. 73)

Chapter 4

College Student Development

Student development theories provide the means to assess how students decide to react to their environment and maneuver through their post-secondary educational process. "This class of theories have been dominated by, but not restricted to psychological 'stage' theories, which posit one or another level of development through which individuals pass in a presumably invariant and hierarchical sequence" (Pascarella & Terenzini, 1991, p. 17). Two popular taxonomies that are used to illustrate the developmental changes of college students include psychosocial theories and cognitive-structural theories. Each school of thought specifies a unique perspective about common issues that primarily traditional aged college students may encounter while describing a process an individual may use as a means to achieve resolution.

Chickering's Seven Vectors of Student Development

Psychosocial theories "view individual development essentially as a process that involves the accomplishment of a series of *developmental tasks*" (Pascarella & Terenzini, 1991, p. 19). Psychosocial theorist Arthur Chickering described in his Seven Vectors of Student Development the linear progression that students experience as they are developing their sense of self and their identity.

Vector 1: Achieving Competence. The ultimate goal of students as they progress through college is to experience increased competency as an intellectual in physical and manual skills and in interpersonal social and personal relations (Pascarella & Terenzini, 1991). "Central to all three is the growth in student's 'sense of competence, achieve successfully what [one] sets out to do"" (Pascarella & Terenzini, 1991, p. 20).

Vector 2: Managing Emotions. Traditional aged college students are often experimenting with how they want to react to the variety of emotions they may be experiencing. "During college, the rigid, reflexive controls inculcated by parents and society during childhood are examined, understood and eventually replaced by internally adopted behavioral standards and controls" (Pascarella & Terenzini, 1991, p.21). Students must identify their opinions and what they credit to be true for them based on their perceptions, whether these perceptions are correct or incorrect.

Vector 3: Developing Autonomy. For many college students, attending college grants them the first opportunity to make decisions about how they will conduct their behavior, while being exclusively accountable for the possible consequences of their actions. "As competence develops, the individual disengages from parents and the need for approval and reassurance and simultaneously reorganizes the importance of others" (Pascarella & Terenzini, 1991, p. 21). However it should be noted that the student may become somewhat dependent on the ideas and personal opinions of their peers and/or group that are interested in being regarded positively or gaining their acceptance.

Vector 4: Establishing Identity. After students are successfully operating in this phase of development, they are striving to realize a clearer perception and gain understanding of who they are as individuals. The existence that they are trying to define for themselves, however, may transform several times throughout their lifetime as their individual experiences in new situations impact them and their sense of realism. However, the individuals who are operating in this mode are somewhat confident about their personal position in their present environment and/or society (Pascarella & Terenzini, 1991).

Vector 5: Developing Mature Interpersonal Relationships.

As personal identity is shaped, an increased ability to interact with others emerges; this interaction reveals

22

'increased tolerance and respect for those of different
backgrounds, habits, values and appearance, and a shift
in the quality of relationships with intimates and close
friends' (Pascarella & Terenzini, 1991, p. 21).

Individuals engaging in the behavior detailed by this vector
are no longer able to operate from an egotistical mode, but they are
not able to consider the needs and impressions of others. The student
comes to know that they will be expected to exhibit some levels of
tolerance while relating with other individuals (Pascarella &
Terenzini, 1991).

Vector 6: Developing Purpose. The students who are
developing purpose for themselves are in the process of recognizing a
number of goals and objectives they wish to accomplish. These
students are capable of identifying what they will require to achieve
their goals both personally and professionally.

Vector 7: Developing Integrity. An individual that is adept at
reaching the seventh vector is able to join various aspects of who they
are and are generally comfortable with the manner in which they
conduct themselves. The student who is operating in this phase has a
collection of personal beliefs and ideals that are coherent and precept
their overall behaviors and reactions to situations (Pascarella &
Terenzini, 1991).

Perry's Scheme of Intellectual and Ethical Development

Complementary to psychosocial theory is the cognitive-
structural theory used descriptively to define college student
development. The heart of the hypotheses within the cognitive-
structural taxonomy is to provide a means to describe how students
relate meaning to their experiences. A model of a cognitive-structural
theory includes William Perry's Scheme of Intellectual and Ethical
Development.

Perry's model incorporates nine points to which a person could
ascribe in order to choose what composes knowledge. The model
"asserts that the developmental sequence of forms 'manifest a logical
order—an order in which one form leads to another through
differentiations and recognitions required for meaningful

23

interpretation of increasingly complex experience'" (Pascarella & Terenzini, 1991, p. 29).

Perry's original nine positions subsequently were divided into four clusters. As an individual advances through the schemes or developmental levels, the individual acquires perspective concerning what they consider to be their personal truth.

Cluster 1: Dualism. A student operating in this position essentially understands knowledge to be something that is absolute (Pascarella & Terenzini, 1991). Answers or wisdom can only be right or wrong or true or false with no exceptions. The student is dependent on the authority figure or instructor to furnish him or her with "the right answer."

Cluster 2: Multiplicity. The student can comprehend that some responses are not absolute when he or she are functioning in this position of the theory. The student can vindicate, even to a fault, that there may be multiple answers that are valid and warrant merit when choosing a response or understanding (Pascarella & Terenzini, 1991).

Cluster 3: Relativism. As the student begins to acquire new insight into his or her own personal set of values and opinions through experience, he or she is also more able to infer that to obtain an answer or understanding may require he or she to designate what they deem to be most plausible. The student begins to understand that although multiple answers may exist, they are not equally valid or deserving of consideration. "This stage can be problematic, however, since the discovery of relativism in ideas and values can lead to a resistance to choose among presumably equal alternatives" (Pascarella & Terenzini, 1991, p. 29).

Cluster 4: Commitment. Students who are in this position of the theory are fully aware of what he or she value as an individual. This type of student no longer blindly accepts the point of views of authority figures or instructors without question. The student chooses his or her own values and beliefs based on their own perceptions and experiences (Pascarella & Terenzini, 1991).

Kohlberg's Theory of Moral Development

Another cognitive-structural theory popular in student development theory includes Kohlberg's Theory of Moral Development. "Whereas Perry's theory seeks to explain cognitive and ethical growth, Lawrence Kohlberg's theory focuses somewhat more narrowly on moral development" (Pascarella & Terenzini, 1991, p.30). The theory designates three levels of moral reasoning or cognitive processes that an individual may be operating in when he or she is obliged to make decisions.

Level 1: Preconventional. A student's decision making may be motivated by the student's need to solicit endorsement from authority figures because they function dualistically in recognizing that their behavior can harbor physical consequences, both positive and negative. The individual operating in the mode is very egotistical, impacted chiefly by the repercussions they may personally experience.

Level 2: Conventional. The individual functioning in this level of Perry's theory is no longer exclusively focused on self, but they are able to acknowledge that other individuals are regularly involved and can be affected by their behavior. Consequently, the individual is extremely interested in seeking confirmation and will respond in a manner that will facilitate this. However, the individual develops a legalistic mentality and "law is seen…as necessary to protect and maintain the group as a whole" (Pascarella & Terenzini, 1991, p. 31); therefore it is widely assumed that all are to live by the rules.

Level 3: Post-Conventional. The individual operating in the post-conventional stage believes they have the obligation to function in a manner that is best for their environment or society in general (Pascarella & Terenzini, 1991). As a result of establishing their own moral code, the individual avoids violating the rights of others and expects others to reciprocate.

King and Kitchener's Reflective Judgment Model

King and Kitchener (1994) describe in their student development model how college students partake in a seven-stage succession of events as they identify their personal truths, beliefs, and opinions. King and Kitchener described this process as *reflective judgment* (1994). "Each stage builds on the assumption and strategies of preceding stages and lays the foundation for higher stages…individuals are not presumed to be at one stage at a time but rather to operate within developmental ranges of stages" (Pascarella & Terenzini, 2005, p. 37). The seven stages of thinking combine to make three specific categories: *prereflective, quasi reflective,* and *reflective.*

Prereflective thinking (Stages 1-3). College students in this stage are generally unaware, unprepared, or unable to accurately recognize, evaluate, or communicate their knowledge, assumptions, and beliefs about issues and problems. Students willingly accept the information relayed to them by whom they consider authorities and reliable sources. As students begin to require more validation and evidence to support the information they are receiving they are likely transitioning to the quasi reflective level of thinking.

Quasi reflective thinking (Stages 4-5). This stage of thinking includes the idea that students recognize that ideas and beliefs require logistical thinking, substantial justification, and reasonable evidence. Additionally, students develop the aptitude to "relate abstractions to one another and to see knowledge as related to evidence and argument" (Pascarella & Terenzini, 2005, p. 38).

Reflective thinking (Stages 6-7). "At its highest stages, reflective judgment rest on recognition that knowledge is neither 'given' nor found but constructed and that knowledge claims are linked to the context in which they were developed" (Pascarella & Terenzini, 2005, p. 38).. Students are able to acquire knowledge and ideas from a variety of sources, and then use the information to establish the foundation for their ideas and beliefs. Students in this stage also recognize the possibility their opinions and beliefs may change or alter as they acquire or are exposed to additional information and knowledge.

Chapter 5

College Classroom Strategies

Lilly and Tippins (2002) identified a variety of factors that students suggested negatively affect their motivation to learn and ultimately detracted from their learning experiences. These factors include the student's lack of interest in the content covered in the courses, an unexciting, unmotivating instructor, an unapproachable instructor who appears unconcerned or uncaring about their students, and course objectives that focus on memorization.

It is to be assumed that if a student were adequately motivated in his or her classes, the result would be twofold. First, students would have enhanced collegiate academic experiences in which the students would have more opportunities to learn. Second, certain instructional problems that exist between instructors and students might be resolved.

Creating Significant Learning Experiences

Fink (2003) believed that the "design of instruction" is most crucial in creating valuable teaching and significant learning environments. However, it is also the element in which few instructors receive instruction. Instructors could vastly improve the quality of their courses if they were informed on how to design their courses properly. The two main areas instructors have influence when designing a course that could result in creating significant learning experiences are establishing a climate in which the students respond positively to and incorporating active learning activities into the course curriculum.

Environment. There is growing evidence that the environment where students are learning can affect student motivation to learn.

According to Archer and Scevak (1998), "there has been increasing emphasis on the role of environmental variable in enhancing or diminishing students' motivation to learn" (p. 205). It would be advantageous for college instructors not only to evaluate honestly the information they are providing students but also to consider changing their delivery methods. Archer and Scevak (1998) suggested that student motivation can be improved by the instructors varying their teaching methods, "The way lecturers approach their teaching, the attitudes and behaviors they specify, is related to student's motivation to learn" (p. 221).

Hanno (1999) believed that the first step instructors must take in order to create more desirable learning environments "depends heavily on honest dialogue among those who are doing it" (p. 323). Hanno further explained how instructors should establish teaching philosophies "based on the view that students are the foundation of the community, thus each individual student deserves to be treated with respect and as an important member of the community" (p. 324).

Instructors may be able to establish a sense of community for their students by providing students the opportunity to become active participants in the management of the course; in other words, students could assist with establishing policies within the classroom governance. Lilly and Tippins (2002) defined class governance "to include those aspects of a course that typically fall under the professor's control (e.g., grading policy, content to be covered)" (p. 353). Lilly and Tippins (2002) and Hanno (1999) speculated that students are motivated in courses that incorporate methods in which students can establish with the instructor the course policies and procedures.

> By involving class members in the class governance process, professors may be able to encourage students to think more deeply about the importance of concepts presented in class and think about whether and how the class can be modified to provide more opportunities to understand important concepts. (Lilly & Tippins, 2002, p. 253)

Curriculum design. Stiehl and Lewchuk (2002) explained how a course could be designed through careful planning to satisfy the multiple audiences that are taking the course. They also suggested that the curriculum should be a "strategic plan with a clear focus and careful alignment of appropriate learning experiences" (Stiehl & Lewchuk, 2002, p. 38).

Stiehl and Lewchuk (2002) offered a solution as to how instructors can realistically design a course. A Course Outcome Guide (COG) outlines for instructors the essential areas they need to consider when designing or redesigning a course. "The COG provides the essential structure for the course...the COG gives the curriculum continuity without taking away the freedom of the instructor and students to learn in the way that best fits their needs structure and continuity without control" (Stiehl & Lewchuk, 2002, p. 44). By completing the COG, the instructor will ultimately identify his or her intended outcomes for learners in the course.

The course design concepts presented by Steihl and Lewchuk and Fink complement each other. Steihl and Lewchuk's COG helps the instructor answer the question "what" should be learned in a course; Fink (2003) helps instructors answer the question of "how" to generate learning in a course. Fink (2003) proposed that instruction and course design should be motivated by methods that encourage significant learning. The goal the instructor has for students in the course will likely dictate which components should be incorporated into the course design. The six components an instructor could consider in designing a course include foundational knowledge, application, integration, human dimension, caring and learning.

Foundational knowledge is a key component to consider in designing a course. This element provides students with "basic understanding of particular data, concepts, relationships, and perspectives, as well as the ability to recall this knowledge in the future" (Fink, 2003, p. 36). Although this component may seem similar to the process that occurs in an instructional paradigm, Fink's approach encourages instructors not only to teach the information they believe students should know but also identify those elements that the instructor believes a student should master as a result of taking the course.

Helping students take what they can learn and applying it to real life situations and scenarios is consistent with Fink's (2003) second type of significant learning experience—application. Within the design of the course, the instructor should provide students with the opportunity to "engage in various kinds of thinking (critical, creative, practical)… [as well as develop] certain skills…or [learn] how to manage complex projects" (Fink, 2003, p. 31).

Most disciplines and/or concepts the instructor wants to introduce within a course are not done as isolated events; they are often connected through ideas and concepts. Integration allows students "to connect and relate various things to each other" (Fink, 2003, p. 43).

Human dimension considers that students should "learn something important about themselves and others… [and] discover the personal and societal complications of what they have learned" (Fink, 2003, p. 31). Students may be interested in entering courses that expose them to issues, concepts, and concerns related to a particular profession or industry. This component can help them both visualize and consider their role and/or position within the profession or industry they are attempting to enter.

Instructors who are invested in their students could attempt to create situations that allow their students to experience learning beyond the traditional classroom setting. According to Fink (2003), there is value in students caring about the information they are acquiring because "when students are about something they have then energy they need for learning more about it or making it a part of their lives" (p. 32).

Fink (2003) described that a key outcome for each course should revolve around the idea a student continues to learn how to grow. A course should cause many students "to continue learning in the future and do so with great [effectiveness]" (Fink, 2003, p. 32).

Active Learning

After identifying the outcomes, the instructor can integrate what Fink (2003) describes as "active learning" components. In general, the instructor can predetermine learning activities and methods that can be included in the course to assist students with learning and achieving the intended outcomes. Fink suggested that, in addition to the standard lecture format that only allows students to receive information, instructors should find additional exercises that promote learning through doing, observing, and reflection (Fink 2003).

Incorporating active learning components into a course does not have to be extremely complex or difficult; it may require additional preparation time by the instructor. There are varieties of activities that instructors could explore. Group discussion, library research, guest speakers, article critiques, experiential learning, and multimedia tools can be combined with each other, even traditional lecture, and instructional methods in order to facilitate learning and even encourage critical thinking. Other examples of active learning could also include case studies, role-playing, debates, simulations, observations, authentic projects, reflective writing, journaling and learning portfolios (Fink, 2003).

Regardless of the method used, the active learning activities should attempt to require the student to think critically about the information the instructor wants the students to acquire within the course. Critical thinking is an ongoing process that allows individuals to expand their horizons as new information becomes available to them. By helping students to become critical thinkers, they can "explore ideas and activities they had not previously considered" (Brookfield, 1987, p. 34). Critical thinking may help students become motivated to learn and explore. In addition "…the capacity to think critically can be seen as one of the chief markers by which we recognize adult qualities in an individual" (Brookfield, 1987, p. 39).

A person's ability to engage in critical thinking is related to a variety of factors; many of which are experiential. "Thinking critically in the context of adult life is, however, a broader deeper activity that involves our scrutinizing the stock of developed assumptions and habitual behaviors we have evolved during our lives" (Brookfield, 1987, p. 37). Critical thinking encourages students to challenge what they have known or are learning, so they can continuously determine their personal truth. The process is one that is ongoing and allows the individual to expand his or her horizons, as new information is made available to them. An individual's growth or development may be greatly influenced by external factors, which will vary from person to person. As a result, "development is conceived as following complex patterns that differ between individuals, rather than as a simple linear progression through a relatively fixed sequence of stages towards a common goal" (Brookfield, 1995, p. 87).

Facione (2004) suggested that specific cognitive skills, such as "interpretation, analysis, evaluation, inference, explanation, and self-reflection" (p. 3-4), are involved with critical thinking. Instructors must understand that incorporating critical thinking within a course involves much more than just discussion between their students. Specific steps or experiences should occur when critical thinking is truly happening.

Critical thinking is an ongoing process that allows individuals to expand their horizons as new information is available to them. By becoming critical thinkers students can "strive to become more liberated from ideas generated in childhood and preserve in adulthood even though they [childhood ideas] constrain us" (Brookfield, 1987, p. 38).

After active learning activities or strategies are incorporated into a course, the instructor should still include methods that assess student learning. According to Stiehl and Lewchuk (2002), "assessments task are what students are asked to do (projects, demonstrations, presentations) to show their understanding and their skill" (p. 51). Students could be assessed in relation to their ability to communicate effectively his or her understanding or reflect critically on the concepts and themes from the readings and how they relate what they are learning to their personal curricula and to their classmates. Students and the instructor can communicate with each other about how they interpret the readings and discuss whether or not they agree with each other's interpretation. This idea is similar to what Fink (2003) believed should happen in assessment, in that "students learning how to engage in the relevant activity, should be getting feedback to help them understand whether they are doing it well or not…good teachers find ways to generate feedback from students" (p. 85).

Dependent on the course, it may be important that upon completion of a course, the student should have a greater appreciation and understanding about the profession with which the class is associated. Fink (2003) described this quality as integration in which the student acquires the ability to "make connections between specific ideas, between whole realms of ideas, between people or between different realms of life" (p. 31).

Chapter 6

The Interviews

Introduction

The purpose of this study was to describe the expectations that millennial generation students have regarding their collegiate experiences. The theoretical framework employed in this study was phenomenology, a qualitative research method that used interviews and personal reports. The researcher conducted in-depth interviews with three millennial age students who discussed a variety of their collegiate perceptions, expectations, and experiences.

Findings and Interpretations

Description of the Participants

The study was performed in fall of 2006 with three students who were enrolled at a small mid-western liberal arts college with an undergraduate student population of approximately 2,600. The students chosen for the study were purposefully selected. The researcher identified three undergraduate college students through the assistance of a mid-level college administrator who was familiar with the research study that was to be conducted. The researcher did not have any contact with any of the students prior to their interview for the research study. All the arrangements for the researcher and participants to meet were made by the administrator who originally identified the student participants.

Each interview was conducted at a location outside of the college's main campus as a means to avoid potential interruptions or distractions. The students were interviewed individually and were unaware of the other participants involved with the study. Each student signed a letter of consent that indicated he or she was in full agreement to participate in the study and allowed the researcher to record, transcribe, and publish his or her responses. In return for their participation, the researcher assured the participants, in written form and orally, that they would retain complete anonymity.

The participants completed the Demographic Data Sheet (Appendix A) prior to their interview; the results are summarized in Table 1. All participants were 19 years old or 20 years old in the year 2006, which qualified them as millennial age college students. Two of the participants had attended only one institution of higher education, their current institution, but one participant had attended a community college for the two-years prior to enrolling in the current institution. Each of the participants lived on campus at the time of their interview. All of the participants classified themselves as being Caucasian.

Table 1. *Demographic portrait of participants*

Demographic Factor	Participant A	Participant B	Participant C
Age	19	20	20
Gender	Female	Male	Female
Student Status	Sophomore	Junior	Junior
Transfer Student	No	No	Yes
Ethnicity	Caucasian	Caucasian	Caucasian
Lives on Campus	Yes	Yes	Yes
Academic Major	Business	Sport Management	History

This study was neither gender nor culture specific. The purpose of the study was to highlight the perceptions, expectations, and experiences of millennial age college students. From the onset of the study, the researcher planned to include only three study participants and did not intend for the study to produce generalized data that could frame and narrow specific expectations that most students have in regards to college. The study's goal specifically focused on the three students included in the study.

Data Collection and Interpretation Procedures

The primary method of collecting data in a qualitative research study is by conducting research interviews with the study's participants (Bogdan & Biklen, 1998). In-depth interviews were conducted at locations outside of the participants' main campus. Each interview was tape recorded and transcribed by the researcher.

Each interview was completed in approximately one hour. There were no major issues or problems that interfered with the participants answering the interview questions completely. Although the researcher would describe each participant as reserve at the onset of his or her interview, the participants appeared to offer increasing detailed insight in their responses as the interviews continued.

The researcher reminded each participant at the conclusion of the interview and in a subsequent e-mail that they had the freedom to verify the transcribed conversation as a means to ensure the accuracy of the data. The researcher electronically forwarded each transcribed interview to the corresponding participant for review, but none of the participants made corrections, notations, or revisions to his or her specific conversations. All of the study's participants responded to the researcher's follow-up e-mail that they were comfortable with the information included in their transcript. As a result, the original transcribed interviews for all three of the study's participants were the primary data used to complete the research study.

Significant Findings-Participant A

Participant A was a 19-year-old sophomore female with a declared major in business administration. Similar to the other participants in this research study, as a high school student she was always under the assumption that she was going to pursue postsecondary educational opportunities. She prepared to attend college after she had conversations with her parents and high school teachers.

> **I just remember that by the time I was a sophomore in high school I really started to think more about it... My parents and teachers and stuff started asking me more questions about what I was planning to do about college, so I guess I started giving it more thought about what I really was planning to do and major in and stuff, I guess during my sophomore year. [1]**

Another activity that made the concept of attending college more real for Participant A occurred when she prepared to take the American College Testing (ACT) college standardize test.

> **When I took the ACT for the first time, and I was filling out the part where they ask you where you want your scores sent to, I remember really feeling that this was real. I almost felt like there could be a wrong answer even on that part of filling out where you want the scores to go.**

Participant A explained that she formed her ideas about college from the information she received from a variety of sources. She reported she was influenced by the college promotional material she received in the mail from various institutions. However, the most significant influences included her attending a college open house, talking with her parents, and her conversations about college with her peers. She chose her current institution as a result of attending an admission office open house event when she was a high school student.

> **I pretty much chose to come to [my current institution] because I attended one of their open houses and was able to get a true feel for how the college worked and everything... they gave a tour and stuff so I was able to see the dorms and the classrooms and stuff like that. I liked the students they had helping out during the open house**

---

[1] The participants responses are highlighted in bold text.

and that really helped me make up my mind on choosing [the institution].

Participant A's parents were influential in shaping her expectations for college. Both her mother and father regularly shared with her positive stories about their own college experiences.

You know my mom talked about how fun it was to live in the dorms and being on your own and making new friends and stuff like that. I really think my parents did a good job of talking to me about how college life kind of is once you get there. They were really happy about talking about stuff, so it made me really want to go and do a lot of the same stuff they did because they seemed to have such a good time. I mean they love talking about it still so I figured it really is going to be alright when I get there.

Participant A's expectations for college were influenced by the conversations she had with her high school classmates.

My friends and I talked a lot about stuff. In high school you know some of my friends had brothers and sisters in college already so they would talk about stuff going on with them. And that made you kind of think about what things were going to be like. I mean you hardly ever heard anyone saying anything really bad about the things that go on in college. You heard that it was hard, but I really can't remember anyone going into too much detail about that. You just always hear about the stuff that people are doing and that really made me want to go and do some of the same stuff.

College learning expectations

Although she was successful academically in high school and regularly received average to above average scores on high school assignments, she initially estimated the academic rigors and requirements of college courses would exceed her high school experiences.

> I really thought the classes were going to be different from
> my high school classes, much harder. I knew I was going to
> have to study to make good grades, and keep a good
> schedule so I didn't mess up anything major...but I really
> did just guess that college would be totally different than
> high schools, so I just was open to the idea that things
> would change to a more advance level when I got to college.
> I guess I knew it was college and it would be harder in
> some ways, but I just figured that if I studied hard and did
> my homework and did everything like I did in high school
> I could handle whatever the teachers wanted me to do.

She anticipated that her college instructors would be different than her high school teachers. "**I really thought that college professors would be a lot harder or smarter than any of my high school teachers, including the ones that I really thought were smart.**" She anticipated her college instructors would design assignments that would require more attention and detail than the work she completed in high school.

> I thought the assignments and stuff like that would be
> more involved and stuff. I really thought that the
> assignments in college would take a lot more of my time to
> do...I just knew that I wouldn't be able to do them last
> minute or anything. That is somewhat different than high
> school, because even for some of the harder assignments
> [in high school] I still could really do them at the last
> minute and still get a good grade.

She discovered that completing assignments in college using similar tactics as she did in high school did not regularly produce the same successful results. Additionally, she understood the necessity of remaining conscious of deadlines as a means to maintain a satisfactory level of work or to balance out the poorer grades received on past assignments.

> Even though I try to plan to work on stuff well ahead of
> when it is due, I sometimes lose track of time or just run
> out of time and I have to work on some stuff last minute. I

mean I haven't received like the best grade in the class when I turn in stuff I worked on in the last minute, but I mean I still get like A's and B's in the class because I got good grades on the test and other things we had to turn in, thank goodness!

Comparing anticipated academic requirements with actual experiences

Although Participant A indicated that her non-academic collegiate experiences were relatively similar to what she anticipated, **"I mean I knew I would be living in the dorms and meeting new people and going to class and stuff. That part I pretty much expected,"** she confessed that the courses she completed had operated differently than she expected. Her initial expectations included, **"That we would take test and stuff, nothing out of the ordinary...[and] I did think that most of the test they give in college would be essay."** She also assumed that she would regularly be required to complete lengthy research style papers. However, she had experienced academic courses that had required students to complete only multiple choice tests, and most instructors provided their students with study guides and reviews prior to the examination. Additionally, she indicated that she had completed only one 15-page research paper, but she anticipated that in future courses she will be required to complete more rigorous assignments in order to satisfy her degree requirements. **"People tell me in a lot of the upper level classes you have to do a lot of research papers...so I guess that stuff is coming."**

She also commented on being inaccurate about estimating the amount of work or time needed to complete assignments in some of her college courses. She was required to be independently accountable for her course assignments.

Something that is really different than high school is the work you have to do for class. Most [high school] classes didn't have daily assignments and homework and stuff. Most of the things you have to do [in college classes] they put in the syllabus and tell you the date it is due. The professors just expect you to do the assignments without

them really telling you what they expect or exactly how to do it. You don't have the constant reminders like in high school. I don't know if I expected the work to happen like that in college. I mean I knew you would have to do assignments and stuff, but it really is a lot more put on you and you really do have to stay on top of the stuff you have due or you will end up missing the due dates and stuff like that, and I know I have had some professors who could care less about any excuse you have about why you didn't have it done. They just think that it should have been done when it was suppose to be done.

She explained that most of her instructors had almost all chosen to design their courses incorporating similar teaching methods. She expected most of her instructors to present information in a lecture style format

You know the professor is at the front of the classroom, they give you notes to take and you talk about stuff and you take your exams on the material. I mean I guess I figured it would pretty much be standard.

She did enjoy the instructors who also incorporated various media resources.

A lot of classes you watch videos or movies about different things. Most of the times they make you answer questions on a worksheet about what you are watching, so you really don't just watch the video. I guess I like when professors do that, it beats them up there talking and talking.

She reported that few students, including herself, actively participate in open classroom forums and discussions. She confessed that she remained minimally involved in her courses as well as with any classroom activities. She indicated when she attended her classes, she was primarily interested in only taking lecture notes.

I do think that the professors try to get everyone to participate and talk more than I would have imagined. It's not a bad thing, but it seems like the same people always want to talk, and the rest of us really don't know what to

42

say. I am pretty bad about raising my hand and joining in on stuff.

Participant A also did not anticipate the amount of group and team assignments.

It seems like most of my classes make you work with other people, which kind of surprises me a little. I know I did it in high school, but I guess I didn't think I would have to do it as much in college.

Although she was open to completing the group or team assignments, her preference was to be graded as an individual because she believed some students did not share equal responsibility while completing group assignments.

Participant A also discovered that some college instructors discussed grades that were lower than what the student expected and provided them the opportunity to negotiate for a higher grade or complete an alternative assignment.

My English professor allowed everyone to make up or redo some of the work you messed up on earlier in the term... Most of the classes you will have to go talk to the professor and see if there is anything else you can do to try to raise your grade if you did bad on something or were going to fail the class. That is something I am use to now, on how classes work, but I really didn't know that things would work like that.

Comparing perceptions and experiences with college instructors

Participant A had one clear expectation in regards to what her college instructors would be like. "I though they would all be super smart...I guess I never gave any thought to them being like real people."

She provided several examples about how she expected her instructors to have high expectations for their students.

You know I was a little scared when I first started taking classes because I thought that the professors would like

43

teach you something then call on you in class and expect for you to know as much as them and then be able to answer questions back. For some classes it is like that, but they aren't covering things that are as hard as I thought they were going to be.

I was really scared to write my essays because I thought they had to be perfect and sound like a book or something...And I did struggle at first, and my grades weren't the best but the professor worked with me during her office hours and she was really detailed on how I could improve so I eventually was less scared to write and my grades improved.

She realized that most instructors expected their students to perform well on their assignments. However, she felt that many of her instructors were primarily concerned that their students initially explore the subject area before attempting to master the subject area.

I really like the professors who open your eyes to stuff and try to show you a new point of view. I know I expected that about college, that I would be taught new things and learn to think about things and make up my mind about what I believe.

Her experiences had been limited with instructors who had incorporated a great deal of technology into their teaching methods and classroom management. Participant A described that the only technology that consistently was incorporated by her instructors was electronic mail or e-mail communication; however she explained how she would be interested in instructors using additional methods of communication to improve the communication channels between the instructors and their students.

I have e-mailed professors where attendance is mandatory to tell them I couldn't make it to class...but I never really have had to e-mail a professor about anything else related to class. I wish they would [use Instant Messenger]. You could ask them questions like right before a test or something...it would be nice to see they are online just in

case you get confused about something or have a question about something.

Participant A believed that it was reasonable for instructors to allow students to use internet resources when completing assignments.

I am use to looking stuff up on the internet...I know the library has the books and stuff in there that is good, but I just would rather use the internet and work from there. I mean that's what everyone does to get information so I wouldn't understand why you couldn't use it to complete a paper for school.

When specifically asked if instructors should entertain their students she did not agree it was necessary.

I don't know about entertain, but I don't think it hurts anyone if they at least teach the course with some kind of interest. Some teachers are just going through the motions and could really care less about you and what they are teaching. I don't think there is anything wrong with trying to make their classes really interesting.

She also enjoyed when instructors incorporated alternative teaching tools, like electronic videos to provide an alternative to lecture.

A lot of times I learn more from the videos than what I read in books or from what goes on in class. So if there is a video or something that can help me learn than I am all for that. I don't have a problems with that.

Significant Findings- Participant B

Participant B was a male student with a junior class standing at the time of the interview. His declared major was sport management, a new specialization offered within the Department of Physical Education. Participant B was also a member of the college's varsity football team and had played on the team for three consecutive years.

As a high school student, Participant B confessed that his attention was focused on his athletic prospects rather than his academic career in college.

> I just wanted to go somewhere where I was going to get a lot of [football] playing time so I could have at least a shot of going pro. I didn't really think too much about class and stuff like that, I figured that type of stuff would work itself out in the end.

He had convinced himself, and was still under the assumption, that his athletic ability would make him an attractive to postsecondary institutions and professional sport organizations.

> Back in high school I really thought that I had a great shot at becoming a pro football player. I know it sounds shallow, but it is the truth. I really thought that if I really concentrated on being really good I could make it. I mean I was good at the high school I went to, but I guess I found out that good at my high school is not really enough to get to the big schools and not be like on the fourth string and stuff. I mean I really think I could still play at one of those big schools right now, but you know I am getting over that because it clearly isn't going to happen. But I mean you never know, I could still get scouted going here.

Participant B's perceptions about his collegiate experience primarily have been shaped by conversations that he had with other college student athletes and college coaches. Many of the athletes and coaches had shared advice on how to be successful academically.

> I knew from talking to some of the guys who were already in college when I was in high school they always talked about not taking classes or picking a major that was going to be too difficult. And the coaches at this school and some of the other schools I was looking at really talked about majoring in sport management or business or P.E. [physical education] or something like that since the classes wouldn't be really difficult and make it hard to concentrate on playing. So I just figured that would be

what I would do. When I started here they had just started the sport management major so I picked it as a major.

Collegiate learning expectations

Participant B explained that when he was a high school student, he was not tremendously concerned about what his collegiate academic life would include. However, as a high school student, he remembered giving some thought to the fact that he would have to pay some attention to his academics in college so he could remain eligible to participate in school sponsored athletic activities. **"You know, I just want to play and do whatever it takes to put me in the position to play. I have always been like that, even in high school".**

He recalled that as a high school student, he did not believe that once he was a college student it would be an overwhelming task for him to manage academics and athletics. He had developed this confidence by anticipating an experience similar to other athletes he had known in high school who had gone on to play in college. His predecessors appeared to be managing their academic obligations successfully.

> **I figured it wouldn't be so bad balancing classes and football because I know a whole lot of guys dumber than me who are still in college and playing football so I remember thinking it couldn't be all that bad.**

As a result, he remained assured as a high school student that like his counterparts, he would successfully meet his obligations as a college student-athlete.

He admitted that as a college student he continued to focus his attention on his athletic commitments and continued to place his academic obligations secondary.

> **It's kind of hard to do a lot of things sometimes that you have to do with classes, especially when we are in season. I mean I hate to say it, but really I need to concentrate on what we are trying to accomplish during the season. I mean I will just catch up with stuff once the season is over.**

Comparing anticipated academic requirements with actual experiences

On a variety of occasions while being recruited as a high school athlete, Participant B was provided the opportunity to witness firsthand the lived experiences of several college student-athletes.

> **When I would visit the schools that were recruiting me they always had you met or stay with other athletes and they never seemed stressed about their school work and stuff so I really didn't expect for it to be all that bad. It's just a part of college, going to class and all.**

Participant B admitted that he initially was interested in becoming a business major after he enrolled in college; however, he declared the sport management major because of the perception that the major incorporated fewer rigorous requirements.

> **I heard about [sport management] before I got here, but not a lot. I mean when I did hear about it being a major I knew that I would like to do that than majoring in something hard or something I wasn't interested in.**

Sport management majors are required to complete some general business courses as part of the sport management major requirements. Participant B stated that the classes included in the actual business curriculum were more academically challenging than the sport management classes. However, he perceived he could benefit from the knowledge he gained in his challenging classes.

> **You know I have to take some business classes and those are hard. But you know, I think that if I decided to work in sports than I mean, you need to know sports and what goes on in it.**

One area that he has some difficulty in managing his obligations successfully involved group class assignments. A number of Participant B's classes had incorporated group work as part of the course requirements.

> **Pretty much all my main classes [have required group assignments]. I know that all the sport management classes**

make you do just group projects and the test. Now that I think about it, maybe just one or two, like my freshman English and my two math classes really have been the only classes that didn't have group work.

In high school, Participant B's teachers had designed their courses so students could successfully complete their group projects during the designated class time. Participant B found it difficult to juggle his athletic commitments and outside-of-the-classroom group activities.

It is harder in college [to work on group assignments], because you have to meet with people out of class and it is just hard to find a time that everyone can meet and then you may not like everyone in your group, or you may get stuck having to complete a whole bunch of work.

Comparing perceptions and experiences with college instructors

As an incoming freshmen student-athlete, Participant B was privy to conversations about the institution's instructors by talking with other student-athletes who were upperclassmen.

Since I came to camp before the school year started I heard a lot about the professors from the other guys. The upperclassmen were always talking about which classes to take and who was hard, and who was easy. So I just figured it I avoided the people they said to avoid that that would at least make my life less difficult. The guys were really good about warning you who not to take.

I figured since they were the academic type they would be old and uninteresting. I can't say that all my professors turned out to be like that, but most of them are boring. It is painful sometimes to go to classes, especially during [the football] season.

Participant B also believed that some college instructors were guilty of treating most student-athletes, specifically football players, differently than other groups of students.

49

I remember them [upper class athletes] telling me, and I really do believe it since I have been here now for a while, that some professors have it in for athletes. They think you can't do the work in the first place and grade you harder, so you can't win for losing in those classes. So all I try to do is concentrate on passing, because you can't win in that situation.

Participant B explained that part of the reason he believed the sport management courses were easier to complete was related to the coincidence that the sport management course instructors were more lenient in their expectations for their students and were more sympathetic of the student-athletes. Participant B provided a variety of statements about the topic.

A lot of the athletes are changing to be sport management majors. Most of the coaches teach them, so they don't really require a ton of work. And most of them don't talk about stuff that you don't already know. I mean they really like to talk more about what is going on in sports and stuff, so if you follow sports it really isn't the hardest thing in the world.

The coaches kind of know also. They try to help you out where they can, because they want to see you do well and be able to remain eligible and stuff.

I think that's why so many athletes major in P.E., because in that major and in sport management, the majority of the professors are coaches and so they are not going to give you a hard time because they understand the athletes.

The coaches also played the role of advocate or mediator for student-athletes. The coaches willingly talked with the instructors about the options for their student-athletes who were in classes where they were having difficulties.

If you let them know you are having a rough time in a class, they will try to see if they can get you some help and I know that some of them will contact the professor and see if they can help you figure out a way to survive in the

50

> class...I didn't really think my coach would care about
> what was going on with me, but I found out that they
> really do care.

For future academic problems that may arise, Participant B indicted
that he would likely handle the situation by initially contacting his
coaches for them to assist him communicating any problems with an
instructor.

> I really don't know what to say to my professors. But then
> again, I guess it depends on the professor also. If it is
> someone that I think I could talk to maybe I would talk to
> them myself, but I just think more things would happen if
> my coach talked to them instead.

Although Participant B had a preference for classes that were
taught by coaches or are sport-themed, he also indicated that some,
but not all, instructors included elements in their classes that help
retain his interest in the course or independent class sessions.

> I like the classes that aren't all about the professors and
> what they know. I like my classes where it is just laid back,
> it's not all that serious. I had one class where we could call
> the professor by her first name and she didn't really use
> the book and told us pretty much exactly what she wanted.
> I thought that was pretty cool, I guess.

When asked directly about whether his college instructors met
whatever expectation he had regarding their teaching and personality,
Participant B claimed that they were.

> I guess you can say they met my expectations, because I
> just listened to what the upperclassmen said and took their
> warnings. And they were right about a lot of the teachers,
> I guess they met my expectations because I really didn't
> expect much.

Participant C was a junior female history major. Unlike the other study participants, Participant C attended another postsecondary institution two years prior to the current institution. At the onset of her high school career, she did not anticipate attending a two-year community college. However as the time neared for her to apply to college, she and her parents decided it was best for her to attend her local community college in order to take advantage of the lower tuition cost compared to a higher one at four-year public and private institutions. She transferred to her current institution in the summer term of 2006.

> **My parents asked me to just try to go for the first two years because my dad had just lost his job around that time I was looking at schools and they told me they just couldn't afford for me to go. I really didn't have a problem with it after a while since it was only for two years. But I was happy to finally get to a real campus this year.**

Participant C viewed her high school experience as one she believed was typical.

> **I guess I was just an average student, nothing out of the ordinary. I did ok in my classes, I got pretty much A's and B's on my assignments. I made the honor roll most of the time and I took some AP [Advance Placement] classes. But I went to a high school where that was pretty much the norm for the most part.**

She went on to further explain that most of the students who attended her high school would likely enroll in college.

> **Even like the kids who were struggling, they were probably trying to at least keep it together enough so they could get in somewhere [to college]. I mean that was just how things worked in my school. I mean we weren't a bunch of geeks or anything, we were pretty much normal, but I think a lot of us knew we were going to be applying to college in our senior year.**

Participant C's older brother had completed his college degree prior to the time she enrolled. Unlike her experience, Participant C's brother completed his entire degree at a four-year public institution. A variety of Participant C's perceptions about four-year institutions were shaped by the knowledge she had regarding her brother's experiences. **"I have an older brother who was in college before I went and I thought he was living the life!"**

Participant C's her older brother inspired her to remain involved with campus organizations as student.

> **I have always been a very active person, and looked forward to getting involved in some of the campus organizations like my brother. He was president of his fraternity and he really seemed to change, for the better, when he did that. I knew after watching him when we use to go visit him that when I got to college I would try to be in charge of some organizations that I really loved.**

Once she enrolled in her four-year institution she became a member of the speech and debate team and intramural sports and anticipated running for a seat with the student government.

She was attracted to her current institution because it was a smaller institution and she believed the institution could offer more intimate learning experiences than their larger counterparts.

> **I remember when I decided to come here, which is one of the reasons I chose this school, the admission counselor said that since this was a small school there was more discussion the classes.**

Although she admitted that several of her instructors had attempted to involve their students in discussion, many students, herself included, tended to shy away from that type of learning activity.

> **I guess since I have been here and with the classes I have taken, there is some discussion, and its not like the professors don't try, but the students act like they really don't want to talk and so any type of discussions the professor was trying to have usually only includes like one**

or two students, at best. So, I guess the professors just give up and go back to the regular old way of teaching since things don't really seem to go well when they try to get the class more involved.

Collegiate learning expectations

Although Participant C's comments concentrated more on the community college she attended than on her current four-year institution, she provided some examples about how her general college experience compared to what she expected from college while still in high school. The first area she briefly discussed was the fact that she knew she would be required to remain involved and concerned with her academic output to be academically successful. "**I knew I would have to study to get good grades, similar to high school**." She also anticipated a high level of difficulty at the college level.

> **I thought that [the assignments] would be hard. I mean I thought what I was doing in high school was hard, so clearly college was going to be harder...I thought that; I would really have to study for my classes. The stuff I would have to do would take some time for me to complete, it wouldn't be stuff that I could just sit down and automatically know. The topics covered would be more complicated than what we covered in high school.**

Although she indicated that she expected most of her classes would require her to study so she can successfully complete the requirements, she had discovered that some college courses were not academically rigorous and required little effort from her.

> **For most of my classes I can't get away with not studying and expect to still receive a decent grade in the class. But there are clearly some blow-off classes in college that can you can use to lighten your load, where you can pretty much put them in your schedule so you have tie to yourself that term instead of having to work hard in all of your classes.**

She did not anticipate the intense pace that most of her classes kept. She was aware this pace allowed the instructor the opportunity to cover a wide range of material.

> **What did catch me a little off guard, at first, is that they [the instructors] assigned whole chapters to read before you met in the next class. You know in high school your teacher would break up the chapters and you would complete it in bits and pieces, but in college one class usually means that you have to read one chapter and sometimes two in one week and then multiply that by each class that you are taking...I didn't expect that.**

Comparing anticipated academic requirements with actual experiences

Participant C was surprised that several of the courses she completed at the community college challenged her.

> **Community college was no joke, I mean it really is college, regardless of what people may think. I know I worked really hard when I was there to get good grades so I wouldn't have a problem of transferring. I keep trying to change people's perceptions about community college that I talk to, because it is not the easy way to do college or anything. If anything it is more academically challenging. I guess I should clarify that I am not saying that it was on the level of a Harvard education or anything, but I really did find that a lot of was expected of me.**

Even though she talked about being challenged at the four-year institution, she had anticipated the experience at her four-year school to be more difficult than she was experiencing.

> **I thought the level of difficulty was going to be a lot more intense then what I have experience. I mean I have to study and work hard for everything, but I just really imagined myself needing to do a whole lot more to complete the assignments. I mean really most classes just require you to take multiple choice test or to write a paper on something that you choose. A lot of people complain,**

but I really don't because I just expected things to be a lot harder.

Still, she did believe that she was learning at her new institution.

I mean I do feel like I am learning. I mean both here [current institution] and at the community college. I have had to read and learn about things that I never really knew about before...I do feel that I am learning.

Among the learning experiences that Participant C anticipated experiencing included in-class lectures lead by the course instructor. She did not, however, anticipate the volume of notes she would be required to take at either institution.

I also knew I would have to take a lot of notes, and that is one thing that truly has been the case both here and at my community college. I swear I have gone through a ton of notebooks as a college student with just the notes I take.

Participant C was originally under the assumption that her smaller four-year institution would incorporate more academic challenges when compared to the larger state university.

I knew at the big schools like [State University] the classes are so big that they pretty much give students multiple choice test and stuff like that. But I thought when I got here at least that different things would be expected from the students here. I don't know what exactly, I just really thought that students would have to write long papers in their classes or they would have an oral test in front of the rest of the class and stuff like that. My parents always talk about how that was how it was for them in college.

She has enjoyed her classes that incorporated in-class learning activities.

I like the in-class stuff when you do case studies or role playing and stuff like that. Some of the books that are assigned are ok, I just can't stand when you have to read it all in like 2 or 3 days. But it is nice when we get to actually talk in class and not just have to sit and listen to the

teacher. I know we do a lot more of that here than my brother did at his school.

In regards to course design, Participant C described how a variety of the tactics employed by her instructors have made her classes more intriguing and appealing.

I love, love, love when you can show movies or find really interesting articles or readings that really get you to understand the stories you are studying from a different perspective...Textbooks do alright in describing stuff, but if you want to get peoples attention with stiff it has to come alive. I think that is why you actually will find a lot of people like subjects like history and like the History Channel because they finally can hear stories in a way that makes since and they can really see and understand how things were happening and everything.

Comparing perceptions and experiences with college instructors

Participant C entered college with some ideas about what she thought her college instructor's personalities and characteristics would include.

Pretty much I figured that they would stand in front of the class and lecture and talk about stuff that we would write in our notes for any upcoming test in the class. I really didn't expect some phenomenal teacher, like the ones you see in movies and everything. I just pretty much planned most of my professors to be friendly and all, but they would give out a thousand notes, that's what how my brother always described it to me.

Participant C had assumed that her instructors at the community college would not design academically rigorous courses, especially compared to the instructors at four-year institutions.

To be perfectly honest, I really didn't think that my professors at the community college were going to be all that tough. I though since it was a community college that

> they really wouldn't teach me a ton of stuff I didn't already cover in high school.

> I did think that professors at regular college would be tough. I though that some would be really hard and that I would really have to study hard for those classes. I knew from my brother that they expect a lot out of you and make you do a lot of assignments that take a lot of time sometimes, so I was prepared for that when I got there.

She also did not expect that most of her community college instructors would have had completed their doctorate degrees. "**Most if not all of my professors at the community college had their PhD's so they did know their stuff.**"

She described her actual experience with college instructors to be somewhat contradictory to her initial expectations.

> Really most of the harder classes I had were at the community college, not to say that I haven't had some hard classes here, but I really think that I spent more time studying and trying to keep up with things at the community college. The professors here [her current institution] are a little bit more laid back than my professors at the community college.

Although she did not go as far to suggest that the instructors at the community college were better than the instructors she had at her four-year institution, she indicated that she thought they did a better job engaging their students.

> I do think that some of the professors that I had at the community college spent more time with really trying to teach the material so people could learn it. We had a lot of discussions and stuff. It was not like here where you pretty much hear the professor talk about stuff in class and you are expected to read something about it and then take a test on it.

Participant C described that some college instructors failed to maintain the interest of their students. She believed that some instructors spent too much time on certain topics that may not be of interest to the students.

I think that most are actually easier than what I would have expected. I though that most professors would talk over your head and you would never really know what to make with what they were saying. For the most part they talk pretty plain, the problem is that they can go on and on about whatever topic they are talking about and you just want to beg them to stop and move on to the next subject.

Participant C did state that her collegiate expectations, in a general sense, had been met.

Most read off their power point when they are giving notes and ask you questions about the readings and that's pretty much the standard. I knew I would be required to take notes and stuff like that when I got to college. That is the one thing that has remained constant between community college and here.

Summary

The findings included in this chapter provide great insight, and highlight some of the expectations and experiences of millennial age college students. The framework used to discuss the finding emerged from three central themes. Within each theme, the participants discussed what they had anticipated about college life and learning, and then followed up with detailed descriptions about what they had encountered as a college student. The themes included: 1) Collegiate Learning Expectations; 2) Comparison of Anticipated Academic Requirement with Actual Learning Experiences; 3) Comparison of Perceptions and Experiences with College Instructors.

"Collegiate Learning Expectations" addressed the participant's responses to their original ideas about what they thought college would be like, and how they formulated their ideas. "Comparison of Anticipated Academic Requirement with Actual Learning Experiences" provided comprehensive accounts of their early estimation about general academic requirements and compared this to what they had essentially encountered as college students. "Comparison of Perceptions and Experiences with College Instructors" explored the projected and the real type of teaching methods utilized by college instructors. The distinction of academic major, relationships with upperclassmen, and academic career path, each influenced the lived experience of at least one of the participants.

The accounts included in the chapter provided a glimpse into understanding why it is necessary for college instructors and administrators to consider the frame of mind of their youngest students. The expectations and actual experiences included in this study begin to identify that there might be central individuals and activities that can play a significant roles with millennial generation college students prior to and during college.

Chapter 7

Conclusions

The data used to develop this study was generated from interviews conducted with three millennial age college students. The student participants who participated in this study were all enrolled as students at a small mid-western liberal arts college. The study attempted to address the following research question: What does it mean to millennial generation college students when they compare their actual collegiate learning experiences with what they anticipated? Each student described his or her collegiate perceptions, expectations, and actual experiences.

The theoretical framework used in the study was phenomenology, a qualitative research method that utilizes interviews and personal reports. The primary research question under the phenomenological format "might be stated broadly without specific reference to the existing literature or a typology of questions..." (Creswell, 1994, pp. 70-71). The participants were asked a series of unscripted questions, and they were encouraged to describe their collegiate academic experiences.

As the interviews progressed and each student detailed accounts of their learning experiences as a college student, each student clearly articulated and compared how his or her anticipated experiences and actual experiences varied. Although each student had established pre-existing ideas about his or her life in college, many of which were the results of conversations with parents and friends, each found that his or her actual academic learning experiences in college often required him or her to devote more time, discipline, and ability than he or she had generally anticipated.

Summary of Similar Expectations and Experiences

Conversations. Although the participants biographies included very few similarities outside of the fact they were all attending the same institution, the students did share a variety of similar sentiments as they talked about their expectations and actual experiences. All the participants shared the fact that they had shaped their expectations about college based on conversations they had with individuals whom they trusted. Participant's A and C both recalled the influence their parents had, and all three participants talked about how members of their peer groups or close associates also influenced their perceptions.

The significance of the pre-collegiate conversations aided in establishing a positive tone for each student developing ideas about his or her forthcoming college life and experience. As a result, each participant believed he or she had entered college with a good idea about what he or she should expect, and they initially believed they were prepared and fully capable of handling the situations that could likely arise. Each participant discussed how few of the conversations he or she had with family and friends, prior to them enrolling in college specifically addressed the difficulties he or she might endure in his or her college life and learning. Instead, they recalled that the discussions focusing more on social and non-academic experiences.

Challenging Course Requirements. Each participant addressed the idea that he or she anticipated their college courses would be more challenging and rigorous than his or her high school experiences. It appeared that when the students started their collegiate academic courses, Participant's A and C used a "wait-and-see" approach in regards to how they were going to meet their individual course requirements, whereas Participant B was prepared to employ tactics he had been advised as an athletic recruit. Although each participant was under the assumption the academic requirements and assignments would be more advanced than what he or she had experienced previously in high school, none expected to endure problems that would negatively affect his or her academic eligibility, status, or transcript.

As the participants recalled their memories about what they expected to experience as college students, they were also asked to talk about what they had actually experienced. There was the shared anticipation that the students believed most, if not all of their academic course requirements, would prove to be difficult to complete. Although they all had encountered courses in which they felt challenged by the requirements and the instructor, the students appeared to had gained self-assurance about their ability to successfully complete future courses once they began to successfully complete their courses. Although all the participants agreed that they needed to remain actively involved in their courses to meet the requirements, they also discovered additional methods they could incorporate to maintain a satisfactory standing within individual courses and in regards to their overall academic record. Such tactics included taking notes, selecting a major of interest, registering for courses offered by certain instructors, and receiving additional help from instructors outside of the classroom.

Instructors. Interestingly the topic about which the students shared not only similar sentiment but also used almost exact phrasing and terminology were related to their expectations about college instructors. The students had convinced themselves that the instructors with whom they would eventually interact as college students would be extremely intelligent. They anticipated not only being intimidated by their future instructors' levels of intelligence, but also they anticipated an inability to relate with them on any type of personal level. There was also the suggestion that the participants believed their own intellectual inferiority would routinely be challenged or critiqued by their instructors in ways that would make the students feel uncomfortable or uneasy.

Although each shared the initial expectation that he or she would likely be unable to relate to his or her course instructors, several statements offered by the participants suggested that they believed their instructors were at a bare minimum approachable. Although Participant B indicated that he was unable to discuss difficulties he was experiencing directly with his course instructor and that he preferred to use an athletic coach as a mediator to discuss his problems, he, like the other participants, did seem to realize it was possible to relate with most of their instructors.

Technology. Although the participants were asked specifically about how different technologies were incorporated into their classroom experience, learning activities, and means of communication with their instructors outside of the classroom, none of the participants were particularly concerned as to whether or not instructors integrated existing technologies into their course design. It did not appear that the students had an initial expectation that their instructors would incorporate such available technologies into their teaching methods. The participants were prepared to attend classes that relied heavily on a traditional lecture-style format.

The preferred teaching format of the student's involved them watching topic related videos during class time. The students did not explicitly express that they initially expected that their instructors should incorporate entertaining activities into their course design. However, there were a variety of comments that suggested how the instructors who did provide some type of entertaining activity, such as incorporating videos of movies and television shows related to the topic, were the activities that they preferred .

For the students with courses in which the instructor incorporated the software program "Blackboard" into the course design, it appeared that most of the instructors used a minimal amount of the software's capabilities and required the students to use very few of the software features. The students did not perceive the software as enhancing their learning experience or ability to communicate with the instructor to a point where they would insist other instructors use the same or similar software in future courses. Additionally, the students did not report that they had expected their instructors to use any other type of software or communication devices or methods.

Group Learning Activities. Several comments focused on the amount of group work that courses required. The students appeared to be familiar with learning activities that involved group work; however, they did not appear to anticipate the number of courses that would require group activities. Although the students described group activities as somewhat commonplace in their college experience, they did believe that the assignments presented a variety of challenges.

Class Discussions. The students were also aware that many instructors were interested in their students actively participating in course discussions. A variety of statements offered by the participants indicated their lack of interest or discouragement to participate in classroom discussion. Although there was an expressed desire by the students for instructors to find alternatives from lectures, the students favored methods that did not require or reduced the possibility of them having to be actively involved participants.

Comparison of Findings with Instructional Issues

College instructors will relentlessly be required to confront problems related to their individual students and with students who elicit a variety of behaviors. In this study the three students identified what they expected from their college learning opportunities and what they actually experienced. Although the participants communicated that they were mostly satisfied with instructors who used learning activities that limited their participation, the students also acknowledged that they engaged in behaviors contrary to what was expected by the course instructor.

Attitudes. Students who are described as having an attitude may represent a wide array of behavioral characteristics. Students with attitudes usually possess one of two distinctive qualities. First, the student may demonstrate in their mannerisms and actions an unwillingness to change or adapt to their new environment (Baiocco & Bilken, 1998). This type of student shows no interest in identifying with the mode of operation that may be established and/or emerging in the instructional environment. An example might include students who read magazines or place their heads on their desk because they do not want to participate in an in-class group.

Another common characteristic of students demonstrating an attitude includes those students who may enter an environment with specific expectations that are not met (Baiocco & Bilken, 1998).

Students may act as if they are skeptical or distrustful of the instructor and/or what is being requested of them. An example might include disapproval of an instructor requiring multiple essay assignments in a course, when the student's previous courses only evaluated the students through multiple-choice test.

Students with attitudes can be characterized as having the following:

> A chip on the shoulder, arrogance, and defensiveness…The words of the students themselves, reveal a false bravado: 'I've done this…worked in this field for several year…taken this course…have a relative who…am well above this level…paid lots of money and I expect…my education in my country was superior to that there…I'm above average…you are holding me back. (Baiocco & Bilken, 1998, p. 174)

The three students who participated in the research study likely qualify in varying degrees as students who display an attitude. Participants A and B each commented on how he or she did not consistently perform or position themselves to meet successfully the requirements that would position them to achieve a satisfactory to above satisfactory evaluation by their instructor. Instead, the participants felt they were correct to navigate themselves around the requirements stated and complete their assignments and tasks as they saw fit, including ways that did not meet the specified requirements. Although the attitude that each student displayed in this instance is not visually extravagant, the actions are making a statement about the value the students places on the instructions specified for them follow.

Participant C compared her experiences from her community college experience with her four-year college experience. Her comments indicated that she believed that her experience at the community college was superior to her current one at the four-year institution. Because Participant C was in the process of completing only her second term at her current institution, she may have not fully made the adjustment to her new environment and internally carried the belief that the former system she had to learn to maneuver was superior to the new situations she was being introduced. Although

Participant C's comments are her opinions and were presented as her personal truth, her novelty to her current situation may have resulted in her incorrectly and inappropriately comparing her current institution to her former one.

Instructors would have the advantage of identifying not only how students with more noticeable attitudes could disrupt their courses but also future teaching strategies.

> Expect more complaints about 'unfair' grades, and even lawsuits over 'injurious' academic evaluations, to be filed by disappointed students and their disgruntled parents...Professors will face increasing scrutiny of what values they impart, or appear to impart, in the classroom...Professors could start hearing complaints from parents who differ with their points of view, especially if their collegiate children report back home that they are getting more attitude and opinion than knowledge in the classroom. (Howe & Strauss, 2003, pp. 83-84)

Lacking Confidence. Many students have the problem of not wanting to be viewed negatively or unfavorably or as being wrong in public forums or classrooms. As a result, some students who exhibit the characteristics of lacking confidence may find it difficult to take risk and, consequently, become reliant, in varying degrees, on the instructor to provide direction on their performance related to their class. "For some reason, taking a chance to answer a question in class or attempt an unfamiliar assignment for such students is frightening" (Baiocco & Bilken, 1998, p. 184). Students operating in such a mode present a challenge for instructors who are supportive of their students to act independently, especially in regards to their learning.

Each student indicated that although he or she liked his or her instructors to incorporate varied learning activities, including class discussion, each was well aware that he or she was likely not to participate in the conversation. It appeared that the students were less likely to participate in discussions if they were unfamiliar with their instructor or the subject, or they did not believe they would receive encouragement from their peers. None of the students suggested that he or she looked for opportunities within his or her course work or class time to challenge in an open forum what he or she was learning and to express his or her opinions on relevant topic areas. The students did not confirm that they looked for opportunities that required themselves to move away from their comfort zone and become more active participants in their classroom environment and learning.

Howe and Strauss (2000, 2003) reported in their findings that the millennial generation is collectively confident. However, they also reported that most millennials are not interested in finding experiences that require them to be noticeably different from their peers, even in the classroom. Because this generation finds solace in solidarity, there are definite implications for instructors.

> This new batch of students will be less comfortable working independently an will reveal a tendency toward safety in number— towards conformity—that may be distressing to professors who may recall a very different classroom environment in the 1960s or '70s. Many high school teachers lament that they can't get their students to debate an issue where they can't get their students to debate an issue where they already feel a strong consensus. Professors will have to go to extra efforts to tap into latent creativity of students who, having been 'taught the test' are unfamiliar with taking intellectual risks. (Howe & Strauss, 2003, p. 90)

Elite Groups Requiring Apathy. Some students may believe that they are entitled to special privileges because they view themselves to be members of an elite group on the campus, such as premedical students, engineering students, honor students, athletes, and so forth (Baiocco & Bilken, 1998). The students of the elite group may exhibit condescending mannerisms towards students and instructors who are outside of their group and/or academic program. There may also be a "contemptuous disregard for the standards of other programs, or bullying tactics towards those who treat them like everyone else on campus" (Baiocco & Bilken, 1998, p. 204).

The study participants included an athlete, non-athletes, and a transfer student. Each group communicated that its group was different from other groups and thought that their membership should entitle them to special group privileges. Their perception of a variety of situations was greatly influenced by their group membership.

This research study also revealed how membership to certain groups causes non-members to assess a variety of theirs and others experiences. For example, one of the non-athletes believed that the athletes receive special group privileges, whereas the athlete indicated that being a member of that special group often created problems with being treated the same as his non-athletic classmates. Similarly, the upper-class transfer student did not believe that the institution was correct in its position to provide the level and type of academic advising it offered its incoming first-year student population.

Howe and Straus (2003) indicated that it is vital that instructors understand the significance groups play in millennials social and academic development as they design course activities.

> Teenagers have become more relationship dependent over the past decade…This results in more cliquish, rule-oriented social world—a world in which cooperation is prized, looking after your circle of friends is priority number one, and being 'nice' is esteemed…Having students debate or critique each other's work (an approach that typically energized Boomer students) is a difficult challenge that often misfires among Millennials, especially when staged before an entire class. (p. 102)

Summary of Results

The purpose of this study was to describe the expectations that millennial generation students have regarding their collegiate experiences, focusing on student responses about student-faculty interaction and course learning. The study focused on how three millennial age college students made meaning of their college learning expectations and experiences. There is some evidence that a significant number of members of the millennial generation perceive college as the necessary tool for them to succeed (Howe & Strauss,

2003). In addition, they also report that learning should be results oriented if it is to be a significant experience worthy of their attention (Howe & Strauss, 2003). This dissertation provided an overview of the variety changes that are occurring within the higher education, to lay the framework for understanding the changes that are occurring within the outlook of a group of its newest students, member of the millennial generation.

Final Analysis

The generational groups most college instructors are likely familiar teaching include members of the boomer generation and Generation-X. The boomer generation attended college when a variety of legal mandates required postsecondary institutions to establish new policies and procedures that would expand opportunities to more diverse individuals and groups (Pearson, Shavlik, & Touchton, 1989). In general, the boomer's viewed primary and secondary education as a birthright, and college as an experience for only a select group of individuals (Howe & Strauss, 2000). The boomer's that attended college were most familiar and comfortable with receiving instruction delivered through a traditional lecture format. Additionally instructors teaching this generation typically designed courses that include instructional methods that were relatively they received during their own educational experiences (Dortch, 1997; Howe & Strauss, 2000, 2003).

Generation-X, many the children of first generation college students, were the first generation who believed they were entitled to participate or have access to higher education.(Howe & Strauss, 2003). During the period that members of Generation-X were traditional age college students, and were the majority group on many college and university campuses, instructors continued on with the tradition of using the traditional lecture format to disseminate information. However many instructors became aware that Generation-X students were not interested in learning for the sake of learning. Generation-X, as a group, viewed their college education as the primary means to get ahead professionally. As a means to aid students in practical skills development, more incorporated individual learning activities into their curriculums (Dortch, 1997; Howe & Strauss, 2000, 2003).

There are notable similarities and differences in the collegiate perspectives and experiences of millennial generations when compared to their predecessors. Differing drastically from the boomer generation, the millennial's view college as the automatic next step in their educational process. It is unimaginable to members of this generation that any high school graduate could be denied some type of collegiate experience. Yet similar to Generation-X, millennial's view college as the necessary tool to succeed, while placing more stock into education than even members of Generation-X (Howe & Strauss, 2003). Millennial's accept that attending college allows individuals the ability to significantly improve professional and personal opportunities.

Unlike the previous two generations, millennial's view academic learning as something that should be results oriented if it is to be a significant experience worthy of their attention (Howe & Strauss, 2003). Millennial's are well versed about the benefits of attending college, many have pre-established notions about the experiences they should have while in college, including the experiences they should have within their academic courses.

The study attempted to address the following research question: What does it mean to millennial generation college students when they compare their actual collegiate learning experiences with what they anticipated? The results of this study produced a variety of responses to the guiding question.

Expectation of Advanced Levels of Learning

Although the students had expected and were prepared for the more advanced level of academic learning often associated with college studies, after the participants began their tenure as college students, they had not aggressively addressed beforehand to how they were going to meet their inevitable academic challenges. Prior to their enrollment, few strategies were offered to the students about how they could successfully meet their academic related challenges. Consequently, the students incorporated similar strategies that they had employed as high school students or tactics they experimented with once they became college students. The students did not appear to be upset or unsettled in that they were not better prepared on how to approach successfully their studies and were proud that they had found ways to compensate for their lack of preparation.

Anticipation of Extremely Intelligent Instructors

The students also anticipated limited commonality with their course instructors. Most of the students had anticipated their instructors' intelligence and knowledge on specific subjects would impede any opportunity for them to have the ability to relate to their instructors personally or academically. Although the students varied in their ability to establish significant connections with their instructors, their regular interaction with a variety of their instructors allowed each student to recognize several of their instructors' intelligence as well as their other professional and personal qualities.

Opportunities to Learn Passively

Although active learning experiences help students learn, the results from the study found that students anticipated a classroom environment that would allow them to be passive participants as well. Although most of the students have participated in courses that relied heavily on the instructor providing lecture-style instruction to their students, some instructors did try to incorporate activities that required student participation. The participants were not necessarily interested nor did they enjoy participating in course activities that required them to interact with other students or the instructor.

Good Instruction

There was little expectation from the students for their instructors to incorporate instructional technology. The students were specifically asked to comment on an available instructional software that can be incorporated into a course design, but none of them were particularly concerned that their instructors did not use the software or other current forms of technology in their courses. The students were more interested in the instructors designing courses that included current, relevant, and important information.

Opportunities to Learn

Finally, there was little expectation from the students on the type of subjects or topics they should learn in relation to their degree or professional goals. They trusted that the instructors were assisting them in building their professional foundations. The students did not enter the majority of their courses with an objective they believed should be accomplished in specific courses. Instead, the students concentrated on finding methods to complete required assignments with the least effort and time.

It is important to note that these findings were true of the students who participated in this particular study. Without question, the findings could change had other students been interviewed for this study. However, the findings support the idea that there are a variety of trends present within the millennial generation that instructors and institutions should continue to consider and evaluate as they attempt to understand the preferences of members of their student bodies.

Chapter 8

Recommendations

College instructors and institutions of higher education need to frequently scrutinize the learning environments experienced by their millennial students. The students interviewed for this study communicated that they were not necessarily interested in being catered to or entertained in the classroom. Rather they anticipated and desired their instructors to be authorities on their subjects, in addition to designing academic courses that utilized current, relatable, and relevant information. The students expected from the beginning of their collegiate careers that he or she would be challenged, not overwhelmed, by his or her college instructors. College instructors are advised to explore the possibility that millennial students are interested in participating in educational experiences that allow he or she the opportunity to grow, and help he or she to develop skills that assist them with accomplishing institutional requirements, and aid in his or her professional development.

It cannot be ignored that college instructors face unique challenges in the contemporary college environment. Using traditional methods to design a course and deliver course content through a traditional lecture format may not be, in many cases, be the best method an instructor should utilize if they are truly interested in their students "learning" in the course. As millennial college student expectations continue to evolve and expand, it would advantageous for college instructors to examine the complexities that are now related to teaching in general, and specifically teaching millennial age college students. Fink (2003) believes the "design of instruction" is most crucial in creating valuable teaching and significant learning environments. However, it is also the element that few instructors receive instruction. Instructors could vastly improve the quality of his or her courses if he or she was informed on how to properly design a college course that established positive classroom environments and incorporated active learning activities.

Environment

There is growing evidence that the environment where millennial students learn is also related to the level of student motivation. According to Archer and Scevak (1998), "there has been increasing emphasis on the role of environmental variable in enhancing or diminishing students' motivation to learn" (p. 205). Archer and Scevak (1998) suggest student motivation could improve if instructors varied their teaching methods, "The way lecturers approach their teaching, the attitudes and behaviors they specify, is related to student's motivation to learn" (p. 221).

Hanno (1999) believes the first step instructors must take to create more desirable learning environments "depends heavily on honest dialogue among those who are doing it" (p. 323). Hanno also indicates that instructors should attempt to establish teaching philosophies "based on the view that students are the foundation of the community, thus each individual student deserve to be treated with respect and as an important member of the community" (p. 324).

Instructors can assist with establishing a sense of community for their millennial students by providing them opportunities to become active participants in the management of the course, in other words, students could assist with establishing policies within the classroom governance. Lilly and Tippins (2002) defined class governance "to include those aspects of a course that typically fall under the professor's control (e.g., grading policy, content to be covered)" (p. 353). Both Lilly and Tippins (2002) and Hanno (1999) speculate that students are motivated in courses that incorporate methods where students can establish, with an instructor course policies and procedures. "By involving class members in the class governance process, professors may be able to encourage students to think more deeply about the importance of concepts presented in class and think about whether and how the class can be modified to provide more opportunities to understand important concepts" (Lilly and Tippins, 2002, p. 253).

Curriculum Design

Stiehl and Lewchuk (2002) suggest that courses can be designed to satisfy the diverse audiences that are taking the course through careful planning of the course. The curriculum should be a "strategic plan with a clear focus and careful alignment of appropriate learning experiences" (Stiehl & Lewchuk, 2002, p. 38). For example, a Course Outcome Guide (COG) could be utilized by instructors as a means to assist he or she with designing or redesigning a course. "The COG provides the essential structure for the course…the COG gives the curriculum continuity without taking away the freedom of the instructor and students to learn in the way that best fits their needs structure and continuity without control" (Stiehl & Lewchuk, 2002, p. 44). By completing the COG, the instructor will ultimately identify their intended outcomes for learners in the course.

Creating Significant Learning

Steihl and Lewchuk's COG helps instructors answer the question of "what" should be learned in a course, Fink (2003) helps instructors answer the question of "how" to generate learning in a course. Fink (2003) proposes that instruction and course design should all be motivated by methods that encourage "significant learning". These methods include: foundational knowledge, application, integration, human dimension, caring and learning.

Foundational knowledge is a key component to consider when designing a course. This element provides students with "basic understanding of particular data, concepts, relationships, and perspectives, as well as the ability to recall this knowledge in the future" (Fink, 2003, p. 36). Although this component may seem similar to the process that occurs in an instructional paradigm, Fink's approach encourages instructors to not only teach the information they believe students should know, but to truly identify those elements that the instructor believes a student should master as a result of taking the course.

Helping millennial students take what they can learn and then be able to apply it to real life situations and scenarios is consistent with Fink's (2003) second type of significant learning experience—application. Within the design of the course, the instructor should provide students the opportunity to "engage in various kinds of thinking (critical, creative, practical)… [as well as develop] certain skills…or [learn] how to manage complex projects" (Fink, 2003, p. 31).

Most concepts the instructor wants to introduce within a course are not done as isolated events; they are often connected through ideas and concepts. Integration allows students "to connect and relate various things to each other" (Fink, 2003, p. 43).

Human dimension considers that students should "learn something important about themselves and others… [And] discover the personal and societal complications of what they have learned" (Fink, 2003, p. 31). Especially for courses that expose students to issues, concepts, and concerns related to a particular profession or industry, the students may be interested in entering. This component can help students both visualize and consider their role and/or position within the profession or industry they are attempting to enter.

Instructors have invested in their millennial students can attempt to create situations that allow them to experience the class beyond the classroom. There are values in students caring about the information they are acquiring because "when student are not about something they have then energy they need for learning more about it or not making it a part of their lives" (Fink, 2004, p. 32).

A key outcome for each course should revolve around the idea a student continues to learn how to grow. A course curriculum should encourage many students "to continue learning in the future and do so with great effective" (Fink, 2003, p. 32).

Active learning

After identifying the outcomes, the instructor can integrate what Fink (2003) describes as "active learning" components. In general, the instructor can predetermine learning activities and methods that can be included in the course to assist students with learning and achieving the intended outcomes. Fink suggest that in addition to the standard lecture format that only allows students to receive information, instructors should find additional exercises that promote learning through "doing", "observing" and "reflection and making meaning" (Fink 2003).

Incorporating active learning components into a course does not have to be extremely complex or difficult; it may however require additional preparation time by the instructor. There are varieties of activities that instructors could explore. Group discussion, library research, guest speakers, article critiques, experiential learning, and multimedia tools can be combined with each other, even traditional lecture, and instructional methods in order to facilitate learning and even encourage critical thinking. Other examples of active learning could also include case studies, role-playing, debates, simulations, observations, authentic projects, reflective writing, journaling and learning portfolios (Fink, 2003).

Regardless of the method utilized, the active learning activities should attempt to require the student to think critically about the information the instructor wants the students to acquire within the course. Critical thinking is an ongoing process that allows individuals to expand their horizons as new information become available to them. By helping students to become critical thinkers, he or she can "explore ideas and activities they had not previously considered" (Brookfield, 1987, p. 34). Critical thinking may help students become motivated to learn and explore, in addition "...the capacity to think critically can be seen as one of the chief markers by which we recognize adult qualities in an individual" (Brookfield, 1987, p. 39).

A person's ability to engage in critical thinking is related to a variety of factors. "Thinking critically in the context of adult life is, however, a broader deeper activity that involves our scrutinizing the stock of developed assumptions and habitual behaviors we have evolved during our lives" (Brookfield, 1987, p. 37). Critical thinking encourages students to challenge what they have known or are learning, so they can continuously determine their personal truth. The process is one that is ongoing and allows the individual to expand their horizons, as new information is made available to them. An individual's growth or development may be greatly influenced by external factors, which will vary from person to person, and as a result "development is conceived as following complex patterns that differ between individuals, rather than as a simple linear progression through a relatively fixed sequence of stages towards a common goal" (Brookfield, 1995, p. 87).

Facione (2004) suggest that specific cognitive skills are involved with critical thinking including "interpretation, analysis, evaluation, inference, explanation, and self-reflection" (p. 3-4). Instructors must understand that incorporating critical thinking within a course involves much more than just discussion between their students, specific steps or experiences should occur when critical thinking is truly happening.

Critical thinking is an ongoing process that allows individuals to expand their horizons, as new information is available to them. By helping students become critical thinkers, students can "strive to become more liberated from ideas generated in childhood and preserve in adulthood even though they [childhood ideas] constrain us" (Brookfield, 1987, p. 38).

Once the active learning activities or strategies have been incorporated into a course, the instructor should still include methods that analyze if students are learning. According to Stiehl and Lewchuk (2002) "assessment task are what students are asked to do (projects, demonstrations, presentations) to show their understanding and their skill (p. 51). Students in a course could be assessed in relation to their ability to effectively communicate their understanding or critically reflect on the concepts and themes from the readings, and how they relate what they are learning to their personal curricula and then their classmates. Students and the instructor can communicate with each other about how they interpret the readings, and whether or not they agree with each other's interpretation. This is similar to what Fink (2003) believes should happen in assessment, in that "students learning how to engage in the relevant activity, should be getting feedback to help them understand whether they are doing it well or not...good teachers find ways to generate feedback from students" (p. 85).

Dependent on the course, it may be important that upon completion of a course, the student has a greater appreciation and understanding about the profession it is associated. Fink (2003) describes this quality as integration of which the student acquires the ability to "make connections between specific ideas, between whole realms of ideas, between people or between different realms of life" (p. 31).

Forecast and Vision

Preparing a forecast, as described by Alexander and Serfass (1999) involves "drafting a vision of what the organization may be like in 5 to 10 years form now" (p. 56). The forecast for the college instructors who teach members of the Millennial generation, which will encompass the next 10 to 15 years, needs to include a vision where instructors move away from tried-and-true methods of classroom management and teaching styles. Instructors will need to incorporate classroom management and teaching strategies that create active learning environments for their students, as well as design course curriculums that truly do follow the spirit of student-centered learning.

The vision for college instructors must always consider at least three components. First, initial change happens with the instructor. The instructor must have the desire to improve the learning environment for their students.

Second, institutions must be supportive of their instructors who are attempting to align their curriculums with the learning styles and preferences of their students. Institutions must be able to provide instructors with resources and support.

And finally, instructors must honestly evaluate how they are requiring their students to learn information. Instructors must be open to varying their teaching methods and instructional styles.

Appendix
Study Methodology

Qualitative versus Quantitative Research

Qualitative research and quantitative research are two very different research paradigms that can both be utilized independently or jointly as a means for the researcher to gain some understanding about a particular research question. A qualitative study typically involves a research process that will generate understanding to a question based on "building a complex, holistic picture, formed with words, reporting detailed views of informants, and conducted in a natural setting" (Creswell, 1994, p.2). Whereas its counterpart, a quantitative study, attempts to understand the defined problem "based on testing a theory composed of variables measured with numbers, and analyzed with statistical procedures, in order to determine whether the predictive generalizations of the theory hold true" (Creswell, 1994, p.2).

Qualitative research is somewhat a generic term used to describe multiple and diverse research methods used to acquire data that is not easily interpreted through statistical procedures or analysis. Unlike quantitative research, qualitative research is often criticized and/or ignored by some because there is little concern on the defined measures the researcher should engage in before, during, and after data collection, analysis, and reporting (Creswell, 1994).

Research Assumptions

In general, there are five basic characteristics or essential assumptions the researcher must understand to provide confirmation as to whether or not the design of a particular study would be better suited for qualitative and/or quantitative research design. The first assumption, the ontological assumption, questions how the researcher wants to define reality. Performing quantitative research, the reality of the situation must be objective and independent of the researcher. On the contrast, qualitative research acknowledges that reality can be quite subjective and that there is also the possibility for multiple realities to exist simultaneously. "Researchers who use this approach are interested in how different people make sense of their lives. In other words, qualitative researchers are concerned with what are called *participant perspectives*" (Bogdan & Biklen, 1998, p. 7).

The epistemological assumption considers the relationship of the researcher to the study, most importantly the researcher's association to the individuals, situations, and/or elements that are being researched. In quantitative research it is assumed that the researcher will remain distant and impartial to what is being analyzed or studied. However in qualitative research the researcher is often required to develop some type of relationship with the participants involved in the study and/or experience the event that is being analyzed. It may be of great benefit for the researcher to reduce the proximity between themselves and that that is being studied. "The qualitative researchers' goal is to better understand human behavior and experience. They seek to grasp the process by which people construct meaning and to describe what those meanings are" (Bogdan & Biklen, 1998, p. 38).

The axiological assumption takes into account the function that values will have in the study. In qualitative research it is crucial the researcher identifies for their audience their personal values and any bias they believe may have that may effect how they will conduct their study.

The language that will be utilized in the presentation of the research, orally or written, is considered as part of the rhetorical assumption. Within a quantitative research study, the presentation of the study is intended to be formal, utilize pre-determined terminology, and accepted definitions, as well as impersonal. On the contrast, qualitative studies gravitate towards language that is personal, informal, and incorporates definitions and terminology discovered while conducting research (Creswell, 1994).

   The final assumption involves the methodological assumption, or the process that will be used to conduct the research study. Generally quantitative studies are using methodology that is a "deductive form of logic wherein theories and hypothesis are tested in a case-and-effect order...The intent of the study is to develop generalizations that contribute to theory and enable one to better predict, explain, and understand some phenomenon" (Creswell, 1994, p.7). Inductive logic is the predominate feature while conducting qualitative research. Qualitative researchers must be capable of identifying the patterns, relationships and existing theories that could be used to explain the phenomena being studied (Creswell, 1994).

Phenomenology

   There are multiple and varied theoretical methods that can be performed by researchers engaging in qualitative investigation. Miles & Huberman (1994) indicated that there are approximately two dozen possible qualitative designs by which to conduct research. Similarly Miles & Huberman (1994) identified 27 classifications of qualitative research.

   The ultimate goal of a phenomenology qualitative study is for the researcher to comprehend the actual or lived experiences of an individual or group. As an extension of philosophy, traditional phenomenology systematically examines a small number of individuals in order for the researcher to successfully to develop understanding about the tangible or evident experiences of the participants. The researcher is often only interested in identifying and explaining behavioral patterns among the individuals being studied, in addition to singling out any relations of the patterns and potential underlying connotations (Patton, 1994).

   Using a phenomenological approach, the researcher "attempt[s] to gain entry into the conceptual world of their subjects (Geertz, 1973) in order to understand how and what meaning they construct around events in their daily lives" (Bogdan & Biklen, 1998,

p. 23). The researcher ultimately wants to depict the worldview of the participants.

According to Patton (1994) there are two implications that must be considered when conducting a phenomenological research study. The first implication is that the researcher must be focused on determining what the participant's experiences are and on communicating how the study's participants paraphrase their experiences for themselves. The second implication is that "the only way for us to really know what another person experiences is to experience it for ourselves" (Patton, 1994, p.70). Therefore, it is possible to perform phenomenological research while focusing exclusively on the participants and articulately illustrating how they interpret their reality, as well as on the researcher examining the actual phenomenon that is being investigated for the study and providing crucial information about his or her personal perspectives and how he or she interpret situations or events that are a part of the field experience (Creswell, 1994; Patton, 1994).

Where ethnographic studies venture to reveal the way of life, generally of a culture or group, phenomenological qualitative studies are chiefly interested in understanding how individual members of a culture comprehend and assign meaning to the events that occur in their lives. An advantage to the phenomenological approach is that the researcher is traditionally involved with a small number of subjects.

In phenomenological qualitative studies, the researcher is also required to recall and present information about his or her personal experiences prior to and while performing the study. The researcher often includes their personal experiences and impressions as a means to assist the reader in understanding how he or she has interpreted the persons that are included in the study, this is often referred to as the *Epochè* phase. "During the *Epochè* phase it is essential that the researcher eliminate, or at least gain clarity about, preconceptions" (Patton, 1994, p. 407).

The next phase involves bracketing. This process requires the researcher to perform a through analysis of the collected data.

In bracketing, the subject matter is confronted, as much as possible, on its own terms. Bracketing involves the following steps:

1. Locate within the personal experience, or self-story, key phrases and statements that speak directly to the phenomenon in question.

2. Interpret the meanings of these phrases, as an informed reader.

3. Obtain the subject's interpretations of these phrases, if possible.

4. Inspect these meanings for what they reveal about the essential, recurring features of the phenomenon being studied.

5. Offer a tentative statement, or definition, of the phenomenon in terms of the essential recurring features identified in step 4. (Denzin, 1989, p. 55-56)

The data is then clustered into groups that share similar meaning, or bracketed. The researcher will then identify existing themes, describe the experience using textural portrayal (Patton, 1994), and extract the interpreted meaning behind the experiences.

This original investigation used methods and procedures common to phenomenological research methods. The intent of the study was to probe and analyze the perceptions and point of view of millennial aged undergraduate college students through in depth interviews about their expectations and experiences in college. In addition, participants interviewed for the study provided information about how college has helped them prepare for future educational and professional goals.

Data Collection Procedures

The students chosen for the study were purposefully selected by a college administrator. A mid-level college administrator who works in a student service capacity at a mid-western liberal arts college identified for the researcher, three undergraduate college students that shared few academic and extracurricular activities. The researcher did not have any contact with any of the students prior to their interview for the research study. All the arrangements for the researcher and participants to meet were made by the administrator who originally identified the student participants.

The data that the researcher generated during the study focused on the description of the participant recalling particular aspects of their life, specifically their preparation to attend college and how they perceived and understood their collegiate experiences through in-depth interviews with the researcher.

The researcher acquired the data that was explored in the study by interviewing three enrolled millennial age college students. The researcher included highlights of the responses and similar themes expressed by the study's participants.

The Constant Comparative Method

Bogdan and Biklen (1998) formally described data analysis and collection as something that commonly occurs in a "pulsating fashion" that involves the researcher engaging in interviews, performing data analysis and theory development, and performing additional interviews in conjunction with additional data analysis and theory development until the final completion of the study. The constant comparative method encourages the researcher to collect and analyze data from multiple sites and authorities as a means to effectively provide direction for the study by identifying themes that emerge from the data.

The formal process that was used by the researcher incorporated the the constant comparative method six steps. The first step required the researcher to collect the data. The second step compelled the researcher to determine and categorize potential themes, issues or recurrent behaviors that is indicated by the data. The researcher collected data "that provide many incidents of the categories of focus, with an eye to seeing the diversity of the dimensions under the categories" (Bogdan & Biklen, 1998, p. 67). Then, the researcher attempted to write about the featured categories by describing and accounting for what had been identified in the existing data, while also continually searching for additional occurrences. Then the researcher to toiled with the data and identified emerging models as a means to identify social processes and connections. The final step required the researcher to participate in sampling, coding and writing the analysis by focusing on the identified core categories.

Establishing Reliability and Validity

As a means to assure adequate interpretation of the information presented in the study, the researcher included in the research design three methods that have been identified in the literature as procedures that helped establish and increase the reliability and validity of a qualitative study. The first method involved the researcher engaging in multiple encounters with the participant involved with the study in order to collect data for the study. Seidman (1991) strongly suggested that a researcher should engage in at least three separate interactions with the study's participants. The multiple encounters provided both the researcher and the participants the opportunity to focus on specific information during each experience.

This study allowed the participants and the researcher to have multiple encounters through the data collection processes that included: one audio-taped interview that was transcribed by the researcher, electronic mail correspondence that followed the initial interview, and one telephone call between the researcher and the participant's that occurred following the initial interview. The researcher kept extensive notes about each interaction.

The second procedure that was utilized by the researcher as a means to establish reliability and validity in the final interpretation presented in the study involved the participants as a member checker. Stake (1995) indicated that member checking is the process that requires the study's participants:

> To examine rough drafts of writing where the action
> and words of the actor are featured, sometimes when
> first written up but usually when no further data will be
> collected from him or her. The actor is asked to

review the material for accuracy and palatability. The actor may be encouraged to provide alternative language or interpretation but is not promised that that version will appear in the final report. (p. 115)

The researcher provided the participant with a transcribed copy of their interview that was conducted for data collection. The researcher encouraged the participants to make any modifications or additions to the transcriptions and related materials that the researcher used for the final analysis of the study. The researcher allowed the participant to advise her of any alterations that they would like made by contacting her through postal mail, electronic mail, or telephone. The researcher was prepared to maintain extensive notes about the additions and revisions made to the transcripts that were suggested by the participants and specify if the revised responses were included in the final analysis. The participants were not provided advanced copies of the final analysis included in the research study.

The third method that was used to authenticate additional internal validity included the researcher clarifying for the reader any bias that may have been present while conducting the study. Under the section "The Researcher", the researcher articulated known bias that were present at the beginning of the study that may have impacted the interpretation of the data collection.

The Researcher

Qualitative research uses the researcher of the study as the primary instrument for data collection, analysis, and interpretation (Creswell, 1994; Patton, 1990; Seidman, 1991). The researcher's motivation in conducting this particular study was to learn implicitly from the experiences and impressions provided by the participant about the expectations and perceived realities of millennial college students. The researcher was also interested in presenting as accurately the information that was shared with her by the participants in order to assist the reader in understanding the experiences of college students. The researcher was not interested in proving or invalidating any existing theories that may explain the behaviors of the study's participants. Instead, the researcher examined how the participants described their college selection process, their learning styles, and the difficulties that they encountered in the classroom.

The researcher has had extensive exposure to millennial age college students and postsecondary institutions. The researcher has been gainfully employed as a college admission counselor for two institutions and has instructed undergraduate students for over five years at two different institutions. The researcher was also the founder and president of a college admission consulting company aimed at working primarily with prospective undergraduate students.

The researcher's general collegiate experience can be characterized as somewhat nontraditional. The researcher successfully completed two undergraduate degrees in three academic years. The researcher also received a master's degree in one year at the same institution from which she received her undergraduate degrees. The researcher has completed a specialist in education degree and was writing the dissertation in order to satisfy the requirements to receive a doctorate in education.

As a means to address any personal judgments or personal bias during the research study, the researcher highlighted in the analysis phase a description of initial assumptions and view points that could be defined as prejudices or preconceptions. Identifying such attitudes aided the researcher in the additional analysis phases so she could be conscious of the potential prejudices or preconceptions as a means to:

> Enable the researcher to investigate the phenomenon from a fresh and open view point without prejudgment or imposing meaning too soon. This suspension of judgment is critical in phenomenological investigation and requires the setting aside of the researcher's personal viewpoint in order to see the experience for itself. (Katz, 1987, p. 36-37)

As the researcher engaged in bracketing, it was essential she regarded the data independently. "Those preconceptions, which were isolated in the deconstruction phases, are suspended and put aside during bracketing" (Denzin, 1989, p. 36).

Implications of the Study

The intent of this study was to enable millennial aged college students the opportunity to describe their experiences within higher education. The experiences of the participants were studied as a means to understand not only what it is like to be students in the 21st century but also to understand what they perceive should be involved in college and their courses. With the information colleges and college instructors can gain additional insight into who the students are that they serve, as well as understand the importance of actively and regularly seeking information about how their students describe and interpret their collegiate experiences.

Bibliography

2005-2006 almanac issue [Special issue]. *The Chronicle of Higher Education, LII*(1).

Archer, J., & Scevak, J. (1998). Enhancing student motivation to learn: Achievement goals in university classrooms. *Educational Psychology, 18*(2), 205-223.

Baiocco, S. A., & Bilken, S. K. (1998). *Successful college teaching: Problem-solving strategies of distinguished professors.* Boston: Allyn and Bacon.

Beller, K., Weiss, S., & Patler, L. (2005). *Consistent consumer: Predicting future behavior through lasting values.* Chicago: Dearborn Trade.

Bennett-Johnson, E. (1997). The emergence of American crime and violence on the college and university campus. *College Student Journal, 31*, 129-136.

Bogdan, R. C., & Biklen, S. K. (1998). *Qualitative research for education: An introduction to theory and methods.* Boston: Allyn and Bacon.

Bogdan, R. C., & Biklen, S. K. (1998). *Qualitative reserach for education: An introduction to theory and methods.* Boston: Allyn and Bacon.

Brookfield, S. D. (1987). *Developing critical thinkers: Challenging adults to explore alternative ways of thinking and acting.* San Francisco: Jossey-Bass.

Brown, L. I. (2004). Diversity: The challenge for higher education. *Race, Ethnicity and Education, 7*(1), 21-34.

Brown II, M. C. (2001). The historically black college as social contract, social capital, and social equalizer. *Peabody Journal of Education, 76*(1), 31-49.

95

Carlson, S. (2005, October 7). The net generation in the classroom. *The Chronicle of Higher Education*, pp. A34-A37.

Cohen, A. M., & Brawer, F. B. (1996). *The American community college*. San Francisco: Jossey-Bass Publishers.

Creswell, J. W. (1994). *Research design: Qualitative and quantiative approaches*. Thousand Oaks, CA: Sage Publications.

Denzin, N. (1989). *Interpretive interactionism*. Newbury Park, CA: Sage Publications.

Di, X. (1996). Teaching real world students: A study of the relationship betwee, students' academic achievement and daily-life interfering and remedial factors. *College Student Journal, 30*, 238-253.

Dortch, S. (1997). A new generation at college. *American Demographics, 19*, 4.

Facione, P. A. (n.d.). *Critical thinking: What it is and why it counts*. Retrieved October 18, 2005, from Insight Assessment Web site: http://www.insightassessment.com/t.html

Fink, L. D. (2003). *Creating significant learning for instruction*. Boston: Allyn and Bacon.

Hanno, D. (1999). Energizing your teaching: Developing a community of learning. *Issues in Accounting Education, 14*(2), 323-335.

Hashway, R. M. (1996). Young adult citizenship. *College Student Journal, 30*, 435-439.

Hobbs, F., & Nicole Stoops. (2002). *Demographic trends in the 20th century: Census 2000 special reports* (Censr-4). Washington, DC: U.S. Census Bureau.

Howe, N., & Strauss, W. (2000). *Millennials rising: The next great generation*. New York: Vintage Books.

Howe, N., & Strauss, W. (2003). *Millennials go to college*. Milwaukee, WI: Life Course Associates.

Katz, L. (1987). The experience of personal change. Unpublished doctoral dissertation, Union Institute, Cincinnati, OH.

Knight, J. (2003, January 31). Millennial generation: College or bust. *The Las Vegas Sun*. Retrieved January 20, 2005, from Las Vegas Sun Web site: http://www.lasvegasun.com/sunbin/stories/lv-ed/2003/jan/31/514599675.html

Knowles, M. S., Holton, E. F., & Swanson, R. A. (1998). *The adult learner: The definitive classic in adult education and human resource development*. Houston, TX: Gulf Publishing Company.

Landau, S. I. (Ed.). (1987). *Webster illustated contemporary dictionary--Encyclopedic edition* (Rev. ed.). Chicago: Ferguson Publishing Company.

Levine, A., & Cureton, J. S. (1998). *When hope and fear collide: A portrait of today's college student*. San Francisco: Jossey-Bass Publishers.

Lilly, B., & Tippins, M. (2002). Enhancing student motivation in marketing classes: Using student management groups. *Journal of Marketing Education, 24*(5), 253-264.

McClelland, A. E. (1992). *The education of women in the United States*. New York: Garland Publishing, Inc.

Miles, M. B., & Huberman, A. M. (1994). *An expanded sourcebook: Qualitative data analysis*. Thousand Oaks, CA: Sage Publications.

Miller-Bernal, L. (2000). *Separate by degree: Women students'
experiences in single-sex and coeducational colleges.* New
York: Peter Lang.

Oblinger, D. (2003, July/August). Boomers, gen-xers, & millennials:
Understanding the new students. *Educause*, 37-47.

Online Electronic Library & Contemporary Women's Issues
Database. (1996). *Can gender equity find a place in
commercialized college sports? [Part 1 of 7]* [Data File].
Available from Elibrary.com, www.elibrary.com

Pascarella, E. T., & Terenzini, P. T. (2005). *How college affect
students: A third decade of research* (Vol. 2). San Franciscp,
CA: Jossey-Bass.

Pascarella, E. T., & Terenzini, P. T. (1998). Studying college students
in the 21st century: Meeting new challenges. *The Review of
Higher Education, 21*(2), 151-165.

Patton, M. Q. (1990). *Qualitative evaluations and research methods.*
Newbury Park, CA: Sage Publications.

Patton, M. Q. (1994). *Qualitative evaluations and research methods.*
Newbury Park, CA: Sage Publications.

Pearson, C. S., Shavlik, D. L., & Touchton, J. G. (1989). *Educating
the majority: Women challenge tradition in higher education.*
New York: Macmillan Publishing Group.

Popli, S. (2005). Ensuring consumer delight: A quality approach to
excellence in management education. *Quailty in Higher
Education, 11*(1), 17-24.

Sacks, P. (1996). *Generation x goes to college: An eye-opening
account of teaching postmodern America.* Chicago: Open
Court.

Seidman, I. E. (1991). *Interviewing as qualitative research: A guide for researchers in education and the social sciences*. New York: Teachers College Press.

Soper, B., Kelly, W. E., & Von Bergen, C. W. (1997). A preliminary study of sleep length and hallucinations in a college student population. *College Student Journal, 31*, 272-275.

Speer, T. L. (1996). A nation of students. *American Demographics, 18*, 32-35.

Speer, T. L. (1998). College come-ons. *American Demographics, 20*, 40-45.

Spiegler, M. (1998). Have money will matriculate. *American Demographics, 20*(9), 50-54.

Stake, R. E. (1995). *The art of case study research*. Thousand Oaks, CA: Sage Publications.

Stiehl, R., & Lewchuk, L. (2002). *The outcome primer: Reconstructing the college curriculum*. Corvallis, OR: The Learning Organization.

Tang, S., & Zuo, J. (1997). Profile of college examination cheaters. *College Student Journal, 31*, 340-346.

Taylor, E. (1997). Crossing the color line: African Americans and predominately white universities. *College Student Journal, 31*, 11-18.

Weistart, J.C. (1996). *Can gender equity find a place in commericalized college sports? [Part 1 of 7]* [Data file]. Available from Contemporary Women's Issues Database, www.elibrary.com

Index

About the Author

Chrystal Denmark Porter, Ph.D., Ed.S., is the founder and president of College Strategies LLC. Dr. Porter is a self-described life-time learner, who is highly motivated in helping students reach their educational and professional goals. Through the years, she has counseled a variety of students about college selection and success. Dr. Porter has worked in three different college admission offices as a volunteer, aide, counselor, assistant director, and interim director. She has also served as an adjunct instructor and teaching assistant for a variety of undergraduate and graduate level courses.

In addition to her experience in higher education, Dr. Porter has worked for the Denver Nuggets, Colorado Avalanche, The Women's Sports Foundation, The Bonham Sport Marketing Group, and The Ohio University Athletic Department.

She currently is working as an independent college admission counselor with the company she founded, College Strategies LLC (www.CollegeStrategiesOnline.com).

Dr. Porter, a native of Denver, Colorado has attended the University of Colorado-Denver, Ohio University, the University of New Mexico, Florida State University, and Capella University. She has earned a total of five degrees, including her doctorate in education with the specialization of adult and post-secondary education. She presently resides in Aurora, Illinois with her daughter Maya and husband Brian.

For more information or to contact

Dr. Chrystal Denmark Porter

please visit online:

www.CollegeStrategiesOnline.com

www.ingramcontent.com/pod-product-compliance
Lightning Source LLC
Chambersburg PA
CBHW051814040426

42446CB00007B/674